THE BOOK OF CHUCK

Here lies a man
so brave & bold,
the story of his life
forgotten—

A shallow depression,
weeds tangled & old,
the splintered marker
rotten

Chuck, 1972

A Memorial Compilation
Of Poetry & Prose

By
For & About
CB Luetkemeyer III

Edited By
Gene Luetkemeyer

This book is dedicated to
Chuck's wives, Linda and Buttons,
to their daughters, Tristessa and Katie,
and to their daughters' daughters, Talia and Zoe.

A SPECIAL FRIEND

Life, Alive, Being,
       all this passes
so very fast, so very final

Embrace it lightly
       as with a special friend
who holds you during the night

Whisper quietly your bonds
       for life is a lover
held in the night
       sweetly

Not to be taken
       but gently received
as a special friend
       held in the night

Chuck, 1972

CONTENTS

SNOWBALL

Well, here we go again!
A bs snowball,
      an idea snowballing
down the slopes
     of ignorance,
becoming an avalanche
     of lost time—

Chuck 9.27.71

INTRODUCTION

This is a book by, for and about Charles Bernard Luetkemeyer III, known to the world as Chuck. It is *by* him because most of the material is his—the poetry and journal entries he wrote since the late 60's, the scribbling on scraps, on post-it notes, on calendar squares and legal pads—whatever was at hand. It is *for* him because one of his last wishes was that his writing be brought to the light of day. Finally, it is *about* him because of the many anecdotal sketches and reminiscences contributed by family and friends, the addition of which creates an image and understanding of Chuck which no single individual could have had, no matter for how long or under what circumstances they knew him.

It was surprising to me that he wished for his writing to be printed and read by others. Little of it has been read by anyone but himself, for whom he wrote it, as a way to express and know himself and as a way to align his interpretation of life with his experience of it. He never attempted to publish; he had no desire to be known as a *writer*. Yet he saved most of what he had written (a great deal of it, anyway; there are several whole years not represented), and this was found stored in a single brown cardboard box in his house among other items that he had organized when he sensed the end was near. No doubt posterity was a consideration. He wanted to be *known*. Most of his writing screams for *connectiveness* and *oneness*, for release from the isolation of *otherness*, which drove him crazy and made him angry. He wanted more than anything else to be understood, accepted, welcome into anyone's game, to know the rules of it, and to play it well with good feelings all around, but this happy set of circumstances seldom manifested, and he wrestled with his private demons behind the wall of separateness till the end.

An abiding principle of his life, which permeates his writing, was the transient and cyclical nature of the material world: matter into energy into matter, essence into form and back, the seasons of life. He took this principle to heart and had a difficult time relating to other people's mundane attachment to form and appearance (he owned little in his life; he preferred the mojo of personalized objects created by and given by friends to the status of passing fashion; he would not stand in line to see the latest popular movie; he despised shopping malls, he found them laughable and depressing, he shopped at Good Will till the end). He became increasingly cynical, sometimes bitter and belligerent, but he never lost hope, never despaired of knowing, though he searched in drunkenness, his preferred state for plumbing the depths.

A few words about organizing and editing of the material. Chronological seemed best because most of his writing, though not all, was dated. Within a given part of the book, identified by span of years, are to be found his poetry and journal entries dated that year, and those not dated but which seemed to come from that period, as well as pictures from that period, and anecdotal material from family and friends who knew him at that time. I tried for a resonant pairing of a piece of his writing with a picture from that period or with what others had to say about him. This necessitated occasionally presenting his work out of chronological order. Punctuation and formatting was a challenge. His stuff was written by hand, quickly, and rarely edited afterward, on all sizes and shapes of paper. It was soon evident that the appearance of his pieces did not translate well to the electronically word-processed format, so some concessions were made in regard to indents, margins, sentence breaks, etc. Most titles of his pieces were supplied by me, for organizational and referencing purposes. Had he gone back through his work for the purpose of preparing to publish, he might have enjoyed, as I did, the process of choosing titles that capture the essence of each piece. Some punctuation revisions were necessary because, in the creative haste of his writing, and in the absence of editing afterwards, inconsistencies abounded. It was attempted at all times to render his meaning clear and not to override his artistic intentions. I hope I was successful. If not, I'll see him again, and I'll hear about it.

Gene Luetkemeyer
Editor, Brother
San Francisco, CA
May 27, 2008

THE BOOK OF CHUCK

The Early Days

1946 – 1964

Photographs
Birth Certificate • Baptism Certificate
Bede Remembers: *Defiant At An Early Age*
Luke Remembers: *Broken Tooth Blues; Motorcycle Blues*
Gene Remembers: *Holding On Tight; Forearms Across The Table; Blood
In The Dust*
□□□

BOOK OF BLANK SPACE

Dark black lines
      definition
soft quiet hues
      subtle touches

Life is a picture
      traced in crayola
by a child
      in a mandala coloring book

A quiet city park
      weathered benches
as stages on the way

An old man
      puts finishing touches
on scribbled pages

A child opens
      a book of blank spaces
& stares in wonder—

Dad, Brazil, WWII

Mom and Dad, Married, Chicago, WWII

FEE RECEIPT NO.
373553

STATE OF ILLINOIS – DEPARTMENT OF PUBLIC HEALTH

CERTIFIED COPY OF A BIRTH RECORD

FILL IN THIS FORM (except signature)
WITH TYPEWRITER OR LEGIBLE PRINTING

STATE OF ILLINOIS   ORIGINAL
DWIGHT H. GREEN, Governor
Department of Public Health—Division of Vital Statistics

CERTIFICATE OF BIRTH

1. PLACE OF BIRTH   Registration 3104
County of... COOK   Dist. No.

Township
CHICAGO { Road Dist.   Primary 3104
Village
City
*(Cancel the three terms not applicable—Do not Dist. No.
enter "R. R.," "R. F. D.," or other P. O. Address.)

Street and Number, No. 1944 NO. FRANCISCO AVE   St.   Ward.

Registered No.

Name of hospital or institution   Norwegian American
Time at above place before delivery?   same day
(Specify days or hours)

Illinois   COOK City or village   Chicago

3. FULL NAME OF CHILD   Charles Bernard Luetkemeyer Jr.   4. Date of birth 12-25-46
(Month, day, year)

5. Sex of Child   male   6. Twin, Triplet or other   Number in order of birth   7. Number months of pregnancy 9 mo.   8. Legitimate? yes   yes   no
(To be answered only in the event of plural births)

FATHER
9. Full name   Charles Bernard Luetkemeyer Sr.

MOTHER
16. Full name   Claire Frances Yarusinski

10. Color or race   white   11. Age at time of this birth   25 yrs.

16. Color or race   white   17. Age at time of this birth   26 yrs.

12. Birthplace (city or place)   Freeburg, Missouri   18. Birthplace (city or place)   Fifield, Wisconsin
(State or country)   (State or country)

13. Trade, profession, or particular kind of work done, as spinner, sawyer, bookkeeper, etc.   order clerk   19. Trade, profession, or particular kind of work done, as housekeeper, typist, nurse, clerk, etc.   hswf

14. Industry or business in which work was done, as silk mill, sawmill, bank, etc.   C. D. Marshall Jewe   20. Industry or business in which work was done, as own home, sawyer's office, silk mill, etc.

21. (a) Including this child, number of children born alive to this mother?   2
(b) Including this child, how many of these children are now living?   2
(c) How many were born dead to this mother, i.e., Stillborn?   0

22. Mother's mailing address for registration notice:
724 W. 21st Place

23. What treatment was given child's eyes at birth?   SILVER NITRATE 1%

24. (a) Was a blood test for Syphilis made upon the mother of this child?   yes   (b) Date blood specimen was taken   Sept 1946   (c) Name of Laboratory making this test.   CBD
NOTE: Result of the test must not be stated on this certificate.

25. I hereby certify that I attended at the birth of this child which was BORN ALIVE at   4:10P   M. on the date stated above.
Burbragter   Physician

Date signed   12-25-46   Address   3242 N. Pulaski Rd   Phone Ken 4701   Registrar

26. Date Filed   JAN 17 1947   27. Signature,   Norman J. ...
Post Office Address:

I HEREBY CERTIFY THAT the foregoing is a true and correct copy of the record of birth as made from the original certificate of birth for the child named therein and that this certificate was established and filed with the Department of Public Health in accordance with the statutes of Illinois.

FEB 24 1966
SPRINGFIELD

Franklin D. Yoder, M.D.
Director of Public Health
State Registrar

Address correspondence about vital statistics records to Bureau of Statistics

Certificate of Baptism

ST. VITUS CHURCH

1818 So. Paulina Street

Chicago 8, Illinois.

This is to Certify

That _Charles Bernard Luettkemeyer_

child of _Charles Luettkemeyer_

and _Clara Yarosinski_

born in _Chicago, Illinois_ on the

_25_ day of _December_ year _1946_ was **BAPTIZED**

on the _16_ day of _March_ year _1947_

According to the Rite of the Roman Catholic Church

by the Rev. _Anthony S. Jarius_

the sponsors being _Stephen and_

and _Margaret Faba_ as appears

from the Baptismal Register of this Church.

VOL. _6_ PAGE _93 # 6_

Dated _December 15, 1949_

Rev. _James Daley o.s.c._ Rector.

5

Mom, Alex, Gene, Dad, Chuck, Grandma, Freeburg, Missouri, 1949

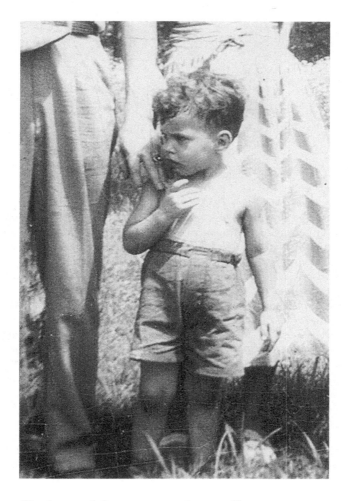

Chuck was defiant at an early age. He got angry at something when he was staying with grandma and said "Damn!" Grandma spanked him good and in the midst of his tears he was yelling, "Daddy says it! Daddy says it!"

Sister Bede, Aunt
St. Louis, Mo, May 7, 2008

HOLDING ON TIGHT

St. Louis, Missouri, 1952. I was four, Chuck was six. We lived on Page Boulevard in a rough neighborhood marked by urban decay. I slept in a little alcove under a window that opened onto an alley that passed behind our block of brick houses. One night as I lay there, not yet asleep, a brick came through the window. I still remember the crash and the curtain billowing inward and the broken glass showering my bed. After this I slept in a single bed in the living room with Chuck. He faced the wall and I faced his back and held onto the elastic band of his underpants for safety and security. One day I was doing something to displease him, or wasn't doing something I should have done to please him, and he said, "If you don't do what I tell you, I won't let you hold onto my underpants!" So I did what he told me to do.

Gene

BROKEN TOOTH BLUES

This event is hard to remember. I'm guessing that I was 10...11? I was still going to Holy Family Grade School. Chuck and I were in the house on St. Leo. We were in the back room. Dad has his watch making desk in the room. Chuck and I were wrestling on the bed. (I probably thought I could whip his ass). I think I was winning when all of a sudden he threw me...or flipped me...or I was just trying to get away when my mouth came smashing down on the bed post. Since that day I've had a broken tooth. It broke in two. Dad didn't have the money to fix it and for years I had my school pics taken with a broken tooth.

Brother Luke
Cahokia, Illinois
May 28, 2008

BLOOD IN THE DUST

Chuck developed a mean streak at an early age. Something simmered, a resentment, anger. Perhaps he felt that his status as the oldest boy was being usurped, that he was not given the love and respect he was due. Whatever the cause, his bullying side was intimidating to his younger brothers, myself included. One day he was harassing Luke, two brothers younger than himself. They wrestled in the dirt under the hot sun and Chuck sat on top and poked his fingers hard into Luke's chest. Luke struggled and pleaded to be let go. I felt I should intervene. I mustered my courage to say, Why don't you leave him alone? He said, You want to do something about it? I hesitated. I was thirteen and weighed in at an unimposing one hundred pounds. He was fifteen and outweighed me by thirty plus pounds, was three inches taller and eager for me to accept. Yeah, I said with a sick stomach; he had finally goaded me into a fight. We were both boxers with the local Police Athletic League and I fancied myself the better, slicker fighter; maybe I could out maneuver him. We squared off and I bobbed and weaved and feinted a few jabs and even landed one to his mid-section. Unphased, he said, Nice shot, then brought his right fist over the top, flush onto my nose. There was an explosion of bright lights, pain, blood and tears. I continued to circle half-heartedly, the blood staining my T-shirt, dripping into the dust. You want more? he said. No, I said, and stifled a sob and turned and walked away.

I felt humiliated for years afterwards, but eventually my humiliation turned to guilt, not because I had fled but because, for Chuck's sake, I should have given him a better fight. He could not have felt good about himself knowing that he had beaten and shamed his little brother. What had he proved? Nothing to anyone, he had brought out the worst in himself and I, by being an unworthy adversary, had burdened him with guilt for his bullying ways that he carried with him always. We never talked about it, but I should have apologized. I should have said: Sorry, Chuck, that I didn't do my damnedest to kick your ass that day, that I didn't make you work a little harder, that I didn't draw a little blood myself, so that your victory would not have been a meaningless one, that you could have said afterwards, Nice try, bro! and patted me on the back and we could have been better friends forever after. I should have but I didn't, and it's too late now, it's just an old faded memory now, just blood in the dust of long ago.

Gene

MOTORCYCLE BLUES

I don't rightly remember what year it was. I suppose it could have been the mid 60's. Chuck had to have had a license. I suppose I must of been 12…13. Chuck had a Honda motorcycle, 250 cc's perhaps. One day when Chuck was gone, the bike took me for a ride in the subdivision. I was cruising along at 20 miles an hour. It seemed like 80 to me. I remember I was on St. Maud. I was coming around the circle and hit some chat when the bike went one way and of course…I went in another. Scratched…battered…and bruised, I got up worried…and hurting…and bleeding. And the bike was also scratched…battered…and bruised, hurting and bleeding oil. I had broken the clutch pedal right off the bike. Needless to say, I was scared now. I knew Chuck was going to kick my ass.

I don't remember how I got the bike home, both of us battered and bruised. I guess I walked it home. I was surprised Chuck didn't do anything when he found out. He was mad, though! For days, perhaps a week, he'd ask me how I felt. I'd tell him I hurt in all the places where I had scabs.

Then the day came. He asked me how I was doing and I told him I was feeling better. The scabs were mostly gone now. After I told him I was fine he chased me till he caught me on the Robinson's front yard. He sat on me while slowly punishing me. He kept pounding me in between the shoulder and the chest, leaving a large and hurting bruise.

I think this is why I have a fear of motorcycles. I have never felt comfortable after that being on a bike.

Luke

11

FOREARMS ACROSS THE TABLE

It was the autumn of 1963. I was a freshman at Assumption High School in E. St. Louis, Il. It was all new to me, the long corridors, the lockers, the hundreds of strange faces. Chuck was a senior. This had been his turf for three years, he knew his way around. A senior! The first time I saw him in the school I came upon him in the cafeteria. I watched from a distance as he sat alone at a far table, eating lunch. He looked bigger then I'd known him, somehow. I walked over. He may have said, Sit down, he may have said nothing at all; if we talked I don't remember, but I remember the sleeves of his blue cotton work shirt rolled up, his thick wrists, the hair on his forearms. I felt him going away. This was his last year, then he'd be gone, out into the world somewhere; he wouldn't stick around a day longer then he had to. And he didn't...

Gene

PART I

1968 – 1972

IN ITS TELLING

Art, poetry, music,
        lines on paper
that are given meaning
        only in the perceiving,
the eye that sees,
        the ear that hears,
these give life to expression—

Man stands in the center
        of the order of it all;
from him flows the music,
        to him flows the art,
                the beauty
that is there only in the seeing—

I want to share with you
        a mood,
        an energy,
something that comes into being
        only in its telling—

                Chuck 1972

PERSONAL DATA	1. LAST NAME-FIRST NAME-MIDDLE NAME LUETKEMEYER CHARLES BERNARD JR			2. SERVICE NUMBER AF17698100		3. SOCIAL SECURITY NUMBER 348	38	5577

PERSONAL DATA

1. LAST NAME-FIRST NAME-MIDDLE NAME: LUETKEMEYER CHARLES BERNARD JR
2. SERVICE NUMBER: AF17698100
3. SOCIAL SECURITY NUMBER: 348 | 38 | 5577

4. DEPARTMENT, COMPONENT AND BRANCH OR CLASS: AIR FORCE REGAF
5a. GRADE, RATE OR RANK: SGT
5b. PAY GRADE: E4
6. DATE OF RANK: DAY 1 MONTH OCT YEAR 66

7. U.S. CITIZEN: [XXX] YES [ ] NO
8. PLACE OF BIRTH (City and State or Country): CHICAGO, ILLINOIS
9. DATE OF BIRTH: DAY 25 MONTH DEC YEAR 46
c. DATE INDUCTED: DAY / MONTH / YEAR NA

SELECTIVE SERVICE DATA

10a. SELECTIVE SERVICE NUMBER: NA
b. SELECTIVE SERVICE LOCAL BOARD NUMBER, CITY, COUNTY, STATE AND ZIP CODE: NA

TRANSFER OR DISCHARGE DATA

11. TYPE OF TRANSFER OR DISCHARGE: RELEASE FROM ACTIVE DUTY
b. STATION OR INSTALLATION AT WHICH EFFECTED: TRAVIS AFB, FAIRFIELD, CA
c. REASON AND AUTHORITY: PARA 2-80, SEC B, CHAP 2, AFM 39-10 (SPN 411) CONVENIENCE OF THE GOVERNMENT
d. EFFECTIVE DATE: DAY 3 MONTH SEP YEAR 68

12. LAST DUTY ASSIGNMENT AND MAJOR COMMAND: 623 ACFT CONTROL & WARNING SQ PACAF
13a. CHARACTER OF SERVICE: HONORABLE
b. TYPE OF CERTIFICATE ISSUED: NA

14. DISTRICT, AREA COMMAND OR CORPS TO WHICH RESERVIST TRANSFERRED: AFRES
15. REENLISTMENT CODE: 1

SERVICE DATA

16. TERMINAL DATE OF RESERVE/UMT&S OBLIGATION: DAY 7 MONTH SEP YEAR 70
17. CURRENT ACTIVE SERVICE OTHER THAN BY INDUCTION
d. SOURCE OF ENTRY: [X] ENLISTED (First Enlistment) [ ] ENLISTED (Prior Service) [ ] REENLISTED [ ] OTHER: AFQT: 8B (83 II)
b. TERM OF SERVICE (Years): 4
c. DATE OF ENTRY: DAY 8 MONTH SEP YEAR 64

18. PRIOR REGULAR ENLISTMENTS: NONE
19. GRADE, RATE OR RANK AT TIME OF ENTRY INTO CURRENT ACTIVE SVC: AIRMAN BASIC
20. PLACE OF ENTRY INTO CURRENT ACTIVE SERVICE (City and State): ST LOUIS, MISSOURI

21. HOME OF RECORD AT TIME OF ENTRY INTO ACTIVE SERVICE (Street, RFD, City, County, State and ZIP Code): 128 ST. LEO DR., CAHOKIA, CLAIR, ILLINOIS 62206

22. STATEMENT OF SERVICE

		YEARS	MONTHS	DAYS
a. CREDITABLE FOR BASIC PAY PURPOSES	(1) NET SERVICE THIS PERIOD	03	11	26
	(2) OTHER SERVICE	00	00	00
	(3) TOTAL (Line (1) plus Line (2))	03	11	26
b. TOTAL ACTIVE SERVICE		03	11	26
c. FOREIGN AND/OR SEA SERVICE		01	03	06

33a. SPECIALTY NUMBER & TITLE: 20330 LANG SPECL
b. RELATED CIVILIAN OCCUPATION AND D.O.T. NUMBER: INTERPRETER 0-68.31

24. DECORATIONS, MEDALS, BADGES, COMMENDATIONS, CITATIONS AND CAMPAIGN RIBBONS AWARDED OR AUTHORIZED
NATIONAL DEFENSE SERVICE MEDAL AFM 900-3/ VIETNAM SERVICE MEDAL AFM 900-3/ AF GOOD CONDUCT MEDAL (8SEP64-7SEP67) AFM 900-3//

25. EDUCATION AND TRAINING COMPLETED
ARABIC EGYPT LANG CRSE NR ABZ203041-041, 65/ SURVIVAL TNG 14000, 67/ VOICE INTCP PROC SPECL CRSE ABZ203480-071, 67/ VOICE INTCP PROC SPECL CRSE AZK 20331-4, 67//

VA AND EMP. SERVICE DATA

26a. NON-PAY PERIODS/TIME LOST (Preceding Two Years): NON-PAY 1 DAY NO TIME LOST
b. DAYS ACCRUED LEAVE PAID: NOT PAID SEE ITEM #30
27a. INSURANCE IN FORCE (NSLI or USGLI): [ ] YES [X] NO
b. AMOUNT OF ALLOTMENT: $ NA
c. MONTH ALLOTMENT DISCONTINUED: NA

28. VA CLAIM NUMBER: C- NONE
29. SERVICEMEN'S GROUP LIFE INSURANCE COVERAGE: [X] $10,000 [ ] $5,000 [ ] NONE

REMARKS

30. REMARKS: HS GRAD/ BLOOD GP O POS/ AQE: G-90, A-90, M-60, E-65, SEP63/ ODSD: 3SEP68/ BI CONDUCTED 3NOV64, 10 OSI DIST/ EXCESS LEAVE 1 DAY/ "I HAVE BEEN COUNSELED AS TO CONDITIONS FOR MY REENTRY INTO THE AIR FORCE AND I UNDERSTAND THAT EVERY FORMER AIR FORCE MEMBER MUST MEET THE ENLISTMENT STANDARDS IN EFFECT AT THE TIME OF HIS APPLICATION."//

AUTHENTICATION

31. PERMANENT ADDRESS FOR MAILING PURPOSES AFTER TRANSFER OR DISCHARGE (Street, RFD, City, County, State and ZIP Code): C/O DOUGLAS BLUHM, 3860 SANTA CLARA WAY, LIVERMORE, ALAMEDA, CALIFORNIA 94550
32. SIGNATURE OF PERSON BEING TRANSFERRED OR DISCHARGED: *(signature)*

33. TYPED NAME, GRADE AND TITLE OF AUTHORIZING OFFICER: HAYES A KIERNAN, 2D LT, USAF ASST CHIEF, PORT SEPARATION SECTION
34. SIGNATURE OF OFFICER AUTHORIZED TO SIGN: *(signature)*

DD FORM 214, JUL 66   PREVIOUS EDITIONS OF THIS FORM ARE OBSOLETE.
ARMED FORCES OF THE UNITED STATES
REPORT OF TRANSFER OR DISCHARGE   1

14

FOUR POEMS FROM A POCKET NOTEBOOK
BROUGHT BACK FROM OKINAWA, 1968

The gypsy brought
        food & wine
to his own funeral
        and danced shadow-like
to the sounds of laughter,
        and having exhausted his
mourners,
        laid himself to rest—

□□□

The wolf has become
        a scavenger,
but fares well off
        the bones of dead kings—

□□□

All the old gods
        are dead,
their graves left
        unattended—

□□□

Droplets of water—
        reflections of past
& wanting for memory—
        A child tries
not to decipher
        nor to disturb
patterns that are not his own—
        An old man will
painfully collect these,
        only to watch them dissolve
into the blur of a stagnant pool
        that was long past
evaporation—

Chuck & Gene, Illinois, Fall Of 1968

ON BEING CORN

It was 1968. We had recently arrived in Illinois from the military, via California. We dropped acid and went out to explore the countryside. We came upon a corn field. It was fall and the field was fallow. Brittle brown stalks were bent over the rows of chunky black earth. We decided to be corn stalks. We sat side by side in the dirt between rows and crossed our legs in half-lotuses and straightened our spines and felt the energy of the earth ascend through our spines, exploding out the tops of our heads, growing us. The air was cold but the sky was blue and sunny and we tilted our faces back and held our arms out, palms up to receive the life-giving energy of the sun. A slight breeze blew, rustling the dry corn stalks around us, but we were vital new young corn stalks, in the spring of life, and we waived happily in the breeze. We spoke in a suggestive, hypnotic dialogue of how we were not mobile, rootless, unsure of our place, but were rooted to the earth. We were, after all, born in Illinois; this was our soil, our home. Why wander? Where else was there to be that was better than this? We ought, like good corn, to waive in the breeze, soaking up the sun, staying rooted on the spot till the seasons turn, and like the brittle brown stalks disintegrating around us, crumble and return to the soil. But the powerful pull of mobility, like a wanderlust, was too great and we decided to rise up and move on, to other new and trippy, phenomenal experiences of the world. But our first efforts to move were unsuccessful. Our crossed legs failed to respond to the commands of our all-powerful human minds. A panic set in as we struggled to extract ourselves from the soil, which had claimed us, of which we would soon be a part inextricably if we could not free ourselves of the delusion of being corn, rooted to the earth. At length, and with a sensation of rending, of wrenching free, we rose up and walked away, with a sense of relief but with a sense of loss, too, of being doomed to apartness from the soil from which we had sprung.

I believe the tone and theme of this experience found their source in Chuck's philosophy and perspective of life, which inform his early writing. Of course, the acid played a part.

Gene

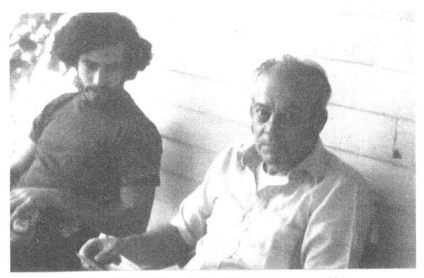

Chuck and Dad, Edwardsville, Illinois, Summer, 1973

HOLES IN THE WALL

It was 1968. Chuck and I had just returned from California after having been overseas and we were staying temporarily at our childhood home, 128 St. Leo Drive, Cahokia, Illinois. There wasn't much to do but drive around and drink beer and talk about what to do with our lives. That's what we'd been doing on this particular night, with an emphasis on the drinking of beer, and we came home late and drunk. Our dad had just returned from work, he worked two jobs, it was around midnight. Soon (somehow, I don't remember the preliminaries) there was an encounter. Chuck and dad stood chest to chest. Chuck shoved dad and said something like, "You never loved me!" then turned and punched holes in the plaster wall against which dad had been shoved. Then dad said in a placating tone something like, "That's not true" and Chuck said, "You didn't give a fuck about me!" then punched more holes in the wall. Dad said, "It's late, let's talk about this in the morning when you're sober," and Chuck said, "You think this is because I'm drunk? This started a long time ago!"

I, meanwhile, picked at pieces of plaster from the crumbled periphery of the holes Chuck had punched and smashed them between my fingers and watched the fine particles float to the floor. I felt helpless; it was beyond my comprehension, this deep emotional turmoil within Chuck whose roots

18

preceded me, some aching father-son rift that I was oblivious to and still am today...because we never talked about it...like all the many things that were never talked about, never understood.

Gene

Without farewell,
    there is no greeting—

Without day,
    there is no tomorrow—

Without pain,
    joy is fleeting—

Without love
    there is only sorrow—

CBL III

POKER AND BULLETS IN DUPO

Illinois, 1968. Chuck and I were living in Cahokia, back from overseas. We were with two old friends, Jim and Fred, riding around in Fred's car, drinking beer, bored, not much to do, nothing new, welcome home. We crossed the bridge that spanned the levee into the back-water township of Dupo and went to a local bar. We drank more beer and shot some pool and Chuck and Fred struck up a conversation with a man, a large man maybe ten years older than themselves who'd been drinking whiskey alone at the bar. I didn't hear the conversation. We left the bar together, Chuck and Fred and Jim and I and the big man, and the man got in his car and we got in ours and we followed him over to his house to play poker for money. We got out of our cars on a dirt road and walked up the road to the man's house, a squat cinder-block house set back off the road in a weedy lot in the woods. It was a hot mid-west summer night and the crickets chirped and the fireflies danced in the humid air. The man led the way followed closely by Chuck and Fred, then Jim. I brought up the rear. Chuck and Fred leaned in close, talking quietly, I didn't know about what. The night seemed to be unfolding without my knowledge or consent; I was along for the ride. We followed the man into his house and down to the concrete basement lit dimly by a single bare bulb in the ceiling. We played cards on a blanket on the floor. We passed a bottle of whiskey around. Chuck and Fred fancied themselves good card players but they were kids, really, and this guy was a shark and he soon had most of our money on his side of the blanket. No one was talking. I felt some tension in the air. Chuck and Fred gave each other a look, I felt something was about to happen, and suddenly the guy says, "No you don't!" He rises up reaches under his shirt behind him and pulls out a big gun and says, "You stupid punk kids think I didn't hear you say you was gonna jump me? You think you're gonna jump me?" The guy squats down and rakes in his money and what remains of our money and stands and stuffs it in his pockets and says, "Don't none a you punk sons-a-bitches move out of this room for five minutes. If anyone sticks his head out the door I'll blow it the fuck off!" He starts to go but Chuck stands up and blocks his path to the door and says, "You're not leaving with the money." The guy looks at Chuck like he's crazy and back-hands him hard with the hand not holding the gun and Chuck goes down but gets back up, his lip bleeding, and the guy knocks him down again but Chuck struggles up and stands in front of the guy. This time the guys fires off the gun into the wall next to Chuck's leg, then knocks him down again, but Chuck gets up a third time and the guy fires another round into the wall. The bullet ricochets off the wall and whines around the basement like an angry hornet. He back-hands Chuck one last time, then bolts up the stairs. Crazily, Chuck races after him, followed by Fred, but the guy is gone into the night.

This all happened in front of me like a dream projected into the world. Forty years later the dream is a bit fuzzy around the edges, but the image remains clear of Chuck in the light of the bare bulb standing up to the man with the gun, getting knocked down, getting up, going down, getting up again, then chasing the man into the night. I saw him from a different perspective from that night forward.

Gene

A MAN

A wolf
   a bear
a rock
   a tree
planted in
   the ground
a man—
   motherfucker!

Chuck

St. Louis, Mo, 1968

ST. LOUIS SANTA

Chuck and I had just returned from California after having been discharged from the military. He got a job at a chemical manufacturing plant in the small, smelly town of Sauget. He worked in an office; he had to wear a white shirt and a tie and keep his hair cut. He lasted a few days, then quit and got a job as Santa Claus at the Famous Barr Department Store across the Mississippi in St. Louis. He was happier there, with a wig on his head and kids on his lap. He liked saying Ho Ho Ho and probably never wore a tie again.

Gene

Cahokia, Illinois, 1969

Back From Woodstock, August, 1969

It was August of 1969. Chuck was off somewhere, I didn't know where. I hitchhiked up to Niagara Falls, New York, to see an old army pal. On the way back, thumbing through the countryside, the roads became extremely congested, streaming caravans of cars and buses. I got a ride in a VW bus loaded with stoned freaks. "What's going on?" I said. "Woodstock, man!" they said, and told me their stories. I couldn't believe I'd missed the show, so close yet so far away. When I saw Chuck again soon thereafter, I told him about it. He said, "Yeah, I was there!" We'd passed within a few miles of each other and didn't know.

Gene

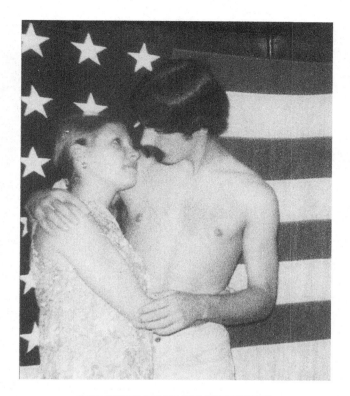

SHACKIN' UP IN CENTERVILLE

It was 1969 and Chuck and Linda and Jim Plate and I lived together in a one bedroom apartment in Centerville, a shabby strip of roadside commerce in Southern Illinois. Jim and I shared the living room, our halves of it separated by a large hanging American flag, and Chuck and Linda shared the bedroom. The landlady, a straight-laced local Christian woman, was not aware that Linda would be a tenant when she rented us the apartment. Within a few days of Linda's arrival we came home to find a note from the landlady pinned to the door. It read: We don't allow no shack-ups! *Immediately, Chuck and Linda went out and found a Justice Of The Peace and got married. They weren't shackin' up no more!*

Gene

25

Linda, Chuck, baby Tristessa, Pacific Grove, CA, probably 1970

Chuck was with Linda and if my memory is correct, I met them when they lived behind Bruce and his wife. Enjoying meals and talking were some favorite times with not only Chuck but the rest of the family members, too. I remember driving Linda to Community Hospital when she gave birth to Tristessa but I can't recall Chuck being with us. We certainly had a lot to celebrate, what a joyous and precious addition their sweet baby girl was…and still is!

> *Michele Jade Sequoia, friend*
> *Pacific Grove, CA*
> *June 10, 2008*

POEMS FROM THE 60'S AND EARLY 70'S
COPIED INTO A NOTEBOOK BY LINDA LUETKEMEYER
A XMAS PRESENT TO HIM

Chuck,

Do you remember any of these? I've collected them for years and thought you might enjoy them. I wish they were still coming. Hope you have a Merry Christmas and a happy birthday.

Love, Linda

P.S. If you see a trip in the future – come east, we have a large house and would enjoy the visit. It's peaceful here among the apple and cherry orchards. Need to clear out your head?

I am the winter of my death
                but not an ending;
        a waiting, stillness of waiting,
guardian of seeds
                in frozen earth—
The storms fall in silence—
        There are no colors,
just white now, unseen,
                still waiting—

But a knowing,
                a change in cycles,
        the turn of time
                Back on itself—
Stillness gives way to movement,
                grass pushes through the earth
        and gives way to flowers—
Death passes into birth
        And I am

I want to just trip awhile in the mountains
& try to mellow out – no dope, no booze,
just walking, growing in the sunshine,
soak up the earth vibes and try to find
a little peace of mind—

Fire watching thoughts –

Sounds of Judy Collins,
        the sweet sadness
                of "Thirsty Boots"

The sad remembrance
        that turns to sweetness,
listening to
        "Baby, you've been
                on my mind"—

My past traveling
        through all the lives
                & all the loves
collapse upon themselves
        like the flaming fire there,
piling into a bed of
                red, dancing coals,

just a jewel-faceted mirror,
        each fiery ember
giving all the warm glow
        of rubies in bright sunlight
or the flush of evening wine—

Thoughts, memories,
        carry forth faces,
                past laughter,
shared secrets
        dance among the flames;
        now, a soft red glow,
and again,
        the flames shooting up
like fireworks on a summer holiday,
        whole memories skyrocket

to explode against the
darkness;
with childlike pleasure
I glow warmly in the sudden light—

☐☐☐

The black clouds split—
look there,
shiny white snow
on Mt. Toro!

☐☐☐

The gate alone remains
of some great Buddhist temple
on this withered plain
(so walk on through
& keep on truckin'!!)

☐☐☐

Spring hills disappear
sinking into the pine grove
as I wander near—

☐☐☐

Living in town
one must have money even
to melt the snow down!

☐☐☐

Going to the country—
you're already there,
& I love you for it.

I am puzzled to see the afternoon
   my mind tells me
     it is night—
I look up & expect to see
   a black sky, dusty through
          the skylight

□□□

Imagining a man, running naked
   through the sprinklers—
hot summer day, in the cemetery—

□□□

The bridge over the canyon
   is spectral, almost nonexistent
in the fog – almost hesitant,
   memory,
like a dream forgotten
   as the sun rises—

□□□

March 71

Just another day,
   not much happening—
Just another day,
   grey skies happening!

Just had a baby girl,
   feeling so strange,
but walking around the campus
   seems no one's changed—

Want to tell them all
   how my mind's flowing,
no one seems to really hear
   what my words are showing—

Not much happening,

30

            just another day—
        Grey skies happening,
            just another day!

                    □□□

FOR LINDA,
        FROM A MOUNTAIN—

Climbed a mountain
        in Big Sur
could see from Point Sur
        to Nepenthes
the sky & the ocean
        and many more mountains—
Was very high!
        Very windy—

I saw many things,
but I couldn't see you,
        and then the sun set—

                    □□□

I though I saw god walking
on the next hill; so I chased
after him, but when I caught
up with him, he was just
someone else's hero, just
another person like me—and
I was kind of sad; I mean,
I had to walk all that way back alone—

                    □□□

3.18.72

I have been gone
        from you
        for such a long time
that there is no feeling
        left in our reality,
just a memory

stretching
down a line of time—

Your face is just a portrait
    set upon the mantelpiece;
friends & events
    are wallpapered,
color and background
    for finer pieces of art—

□□□

3.18.72

I'm so down
    think I'll take a walk;
the sky must be grey,
    though I haven't bothered
        to look—

The ocean is lake-calm,
    no waves to draw me out;
I feel like the slow motion
    of a seagull
as he slips down the sides of air—

The trees in the park
    are empty of music,
it has gone with the leaves
    of last summer—
The winter branches
    are black & naked
    against the sky;
no wind sings there,
    but rather
slips across the grass with a sigh—

3.18.72

My memories have become
   exercises
    in architecture,
attempts & arrangements
   to fix rooms & walls
within this shell I carry
   on my wanderings—

□□□

To be totally free, one must
understand that your actions
are your own and whatever
happens good or bad must
be taken as yours also—

□□□

Past evening time,
   dark night time—

The sound
   of waves crashing,
the memories
   of friends laughing,

I wonder of things
   now & passing!

My only light is
   a candle pressing
the darkness around me,
   like the fog surrounding
the Big Sur night—

"I'M TRYING TO SAY 'I'M SORRY' POEM"

I tried to make love happen,
   Forcing a bond
& ended up in chains—

Held to you & you to I,
   I longed for my freedom
but wouldn't let you go—

Pulling you, like weights,
   or fighting to keep you near,
I saw you only as my prison—

I cut you loose
   not knowing, caring,
where you ended up—

But now I drag my chains around;
   my own ghost, I am afraid
      of shadows
for fear of meeting myself there—

I get no rest;
   the chains rattle against the
      headboards
& keep me awake through the night—

I thought I was growing
      older,
but find that I am just tired,
   so very, very tired—

□□□

The new year begins;
the old has been turned under
to give soil for the new—

The hexagram in the circle is the
24th "return" (the turning point);

it is the symbol for the cycles
of the heavens & earth—

All is reborn; as the river flows
life is washed again & again,
the silt building wide, lush deltas
of green growth—

□□□

1.14.72

So many times
     we first build a shell
and then try to arrange
     our live inside it—

Better that we follow
     the plan of our being
and let the shell grow
     to fit the shape of our life

□□□

Mother's day,
a special day,
spring day
when the grass & flowers
dance to the wind song
and thoughts are mellow
like clouds in the sky—

□□□

Sometimes
     I feel the urge, the need
     to paint, or draw,
     a scene or two—
People hurrying by the library
     seen from this window
     make beautiful subjects
I can paint in the sunlight—

Smiles & cheekbones,
   wisps of hair
and sounds of laughter
   are colors of the wind—
Or perhaps
   I could sketch their absurd
   ego's gestures,
         comic in mime;
their importance of it all
   is lost to me,
separated by the glass
   & the distance,
the shadings of attitudes
   mixed in a pallet of memory,
colors drawn & mixed
   with imagination & experience—

                    ☐☐☐

Without farewell,
   there is no greeting—

Without day,
   there is no tomorrow—

Without pain,
   joy is fleeting—

Without love
   there is only sorrow—

                    ☐☐☐

The sun reaches for
   the high valley walls,
touches,
   then is quickly gone—

Damn!
   I throw a rock
at the advancing shadows—

If the wind
     blew me from this high place,
only the wind would know—

□□□

Under low grey
     winter skies,
water pushes water
     on its way

Sunday, January 28th

Chuck,

Well, my plan was to get this book of your thoughts over the last 9 years to you by Christmas—things always get put off—in the space since then more boxes have been cleaned out—more poetry found. Now I think they're all here. How I've treasured them. Was hoping to have had a letter by now. Hope all is well.

I'm glad Christmas is over and all the bullshit that goes with it. I didn't even fake a Christmas spirit this year, but Santa was good to me anyway. Only got what I needed and a couple of surprises of what I wanted. (Thanks for the little white helpers) Our mild winter I think is over—it's been bitter for a week, the blue skies from this morning are now grey—snow is in the forecast.

Tris is fine. She's not much into letter writing, even though she talks about it all the time. Had a conference with her teacher on Friday. The teacher is pleased to have her in the class, an above average student—a leader in the room. A story teller, a comedian but overly sensitive at times. We finally got our piano, she puts a lot of energy into it. I would like to channel her sensitivity into the arts—I think it's working. Everything is fine with me also—I love my job more and more everyday. I guess it's the responsibility of the two young orchards that I tend. It still blows me away that I lucked into this job and fine house that goes with it. I can't wait until spring to disk the ground and plant my seeds. I am so tired of the brown. Well anyway— hope you're well. Will try to get some pictures to you soon. Write when you can.

Love,
Linda

Chuck & Linda, Pacific Grove, 1970

FOR LINDA,
        FROM A MOUNTAIN—

Climbed a mountain
        in Big Sur
could see from Point Sur
        to Nepenthes
the sky & the ocean
        and many more mountains—
Was very high!
        Very windy—

I saw many things,
but I couldn't see you,
        and then the sun set—

UNSENT LETTER
INTENDED RECIPIENT
UNKNOWN, EARLY 70's

Baby, Baby, Baby,

Just a few words to share the evening with you—I love you!—
Dylan's first album—Freight Train Blues, the echo of the trains on the tracks
near the shopping center—caught up in the middle of staying and going, of
living and dying, of me and you—at times it is a sadness, mellow like
evening breezes and the sound of summer lightening, only to change into the
rage of a sudden storm, swelling up, coming to the point of breaking and
then explosion—the closer I get to finding out where I'm at, the more I lose
myself in where I've been—wish I could stop it all, step outside and just
breath some fresh air—

Bunch of chicks, 12-13 years old, stopped me today, asked if I was Tiny Tim,
wanted to ball me, but saw that I was married and went on back to school—

I see birth behind me, death in front of me—if you look from one to the
other fast enough, you probably couldn't tell the difference—

        I sit upon a lonely star
        and sometimes wonder where you are—

If I could be Steve Miller, I'd play your body like a harmonica, you could be
Joan Baez and learn your chords upon the strings of my body—the whole
world should be a body orchestra and fuck a concerto for god to nod out
to—

        MAYBE is but a foundation for
        the scheme of it all—

Have you ever sat in the same room with the same people, saying the same
thing over and over again and then wonder if you've been there before?
Buddha went to heaven with his eyes and every time he looked at god, he
had an orgasm—some people have an orgasm and see god from the other
side of his eyes—I just read of a woman who could swallow her nose; if she
could eat herself, I wonder if they would have put that in Ripley's Believe It

Or Not—There was a guy who balled a wall socket, just as he came, the wall clock stopped and the guy disappeared—wonder if god ever gets pregnant from forgetting to wind his watch—

Take this letter to bed with you—do a couple of deep breathing exercises, smoke a number, look at some obscene pictures, smoke another number, masturbate, and I'll have a wet dream—a 3,000 mile orgasm—love is all,

Chuck

DREAMING A POEM

Sitting here
    ½ a house above
the Monterey streets,

watching the cars
    come & go softly
into the fog,

a warm, misty blanket
    that gives softness
to harsh city night—

Songs of Joan Baez
    mingle & drift
with grey, twisting smoke

that lifts & rises
    from the cigarette
held in my hand,

a hazy, smoky dream
    in perfect counterpart
with the fog outside my window—

I sit here dreaming
    a poem—

I have a very special friend
    who loves me—

like a spring high up
    in the mountains

forever & ever
    pouring out love,

sweet mountain
    water that flows
across white polished stone

to sparkle in the day
    & sing through the night,

a song for one to hear
    (and to quench ones thirst)
        (and to quiet ones soul)

sweet water that satisfies one
    only for a moment
and then again & again—

Chuck & Linda, 1970, Place Unknown

What can I say? He was my lover, he was once my husband, we were friends till the end...

                    Linda Luetkemeyer
                    First Wife
                    Kentucky, June 16, 2008

43

MYSTERY PLACE

The light sparkling on the edge of
                              a glass,

images that float through my mind
              like carbonated bubbles
                            in my beer
              rising from some mystery place,
                    drifting to white expression
                            on the surface,
                    white foam that disappears
                            & leaves my beer
                                warm & flat—

You are an image that rises
              from that mystery place that
                    is in my past—

DOWN

I'm so down, the sky must be grey
tho I haven't bothered to look—

The ocean is lake-calm,
   no waves to draw me out;
I feel like the slow motion
   of a seagull, that slips
down a current of air—

      □□□

SEAGULL

Music, music
   sing a sad song!

the beat & tempo slow
   my body tires, begins to nod
a physical feeling
   rushes high, the head opens—

Ha! a seagull
   high above the clear sky!

      □□□

SUNSET ON ASILOMAR BEACH

Sunset on Asilomar Beach,
   the cars line up
      close into the rocks
   to watch the end of another day
and as the last part of the sun
   slips beneath the clouds
all the cars start up,
      back up and leave;
leave the ocean like cars
   sneaking backwards out of a
         drive-in—

DOWN THE LINE TIME

Moving one more time,
    moving down the line time,
On the road time,
    thumb-bumming time,
Pruning back to the roots
    time—

Time passes like water,
    flows like the river,
solid, like floes,
    frozen
under dark bridges,
    against pylons of concrete—

Or more measured
    like the sun & the moon,
the seasons,
    winter to summer,
        life to death,
Autumn leaves,
        buds to spring—

FREEDOM

Imprisonment
   is not control—

The freedom
   of a chain
      is no freedom at all—

To deaden your spirit
   is to exist,
      not to live—

To exchange freedom
   for existence
      is to gain nothing;
it is a progressive subtraction
   from the infinity of zero—

         Chuck, 10.78.71

     □□□

DUST

"Dust"
   think of dryness
      a surface laid bare
         to wind & sun

"Dust"
   think of erosion
      the spirit of the land
         laid open & twisted

"Dust"
   think of growth
      the flowering of nature
turned to a struggling for life—

LIFE & BEING

I find it curious
    that in all the words
I've read,
in all the ages from
    which they came,
there is no real difference
    in the mood,
nor is there anything new
    being said
on anything so basic
    as the questions
        of Life & Being—

It is enough to make
    one believe
man is a joke
    or at best
an accident;
    building a universe,
an order out of
    a type of insane
        desperation—

    Chuck 3.8.71

A MORPHINE MOVEMENT IN 'C' MINOR

What can I say
            to turn you on?
        What words could I use
to tell you
        that your troubles are just
            illusion?
Like that set of clothes
        you say covers up your
            nakedness?
How can I lift you
        from this age,
                from your age
        that has settled on you
like the concrete that covers
                so much of the earth?

I ask a few minutes of your time
        for a few minutes of my time—

You couldn't get a better deal than that
        from a U.S. Army recruiter!—

Inexpression
        is self-constipation
                (bullshit)—
Expression
        is a psychic bowel movement
        is as good as balling—

Why do I feel that even though I just
sit across the room from you, that
the distance is so great that if I walked all
day I might never reach you?

There is an answer, though the knowledge
does little to lessen the question—

It is because you are just an illusion,
someone that I have created out of words

& memories of past acquaintances—

Out of my thirst for reality, I have
created you, as a mirage that will waver
forever on the horizon, staying just
a short distance away no matter how
long I try to reach you—

It becomes then
     a matter of interpretation

mouthing sounds,
     like sonar & bats,

using the feedback
     to find our way in the dark—

Pain unasked for is a gift,
     pain asked for is stupidity—
humility in this society
     is asking for a kick in the ass,
but you'll land in heaven—

Chaos is the birth of order,
order dies into chaos—
flowers grow out of the earth
& die into the earth,
autumn into winter,
winter into spring
into summer into autumn—
cycles microcosmic
into macrocosmic
into infinity—
sadness into happiness!
No lines crossed,
just a cycle of attitudes—
Nothing is any different
than something else

Mood & feeling are energies
     subject to laws,
like electricity is an energy

& subject to laws—

It can be understood,
　　at least recognized,
tapped & controlled—

A mood given is
　　mood received—

　　　　Thank you for your time,
　　　　　　Love is all,

　　　　Chuck
　　　　Monterey 9.19.71

MAN IN THOUGHT

A poem must travel along time & distance
much as a train must travel along
        the tracks
or a straight line must travel
            between two points—

A story,
     a truth, is subject to physical laws
         as traveling is to
            time & space,

as the ocean
    is subject
        to motion & pattern,
           to cycle & energy—

The gulls in flight,
       in fluid motion,
    are following currents
         of the ocean,
are subject to its energy
        & its track
          in passing—

So is man in thought
         & thinking,
    in past & present,
        the inevitability,
the passing energy
    that becomes
        the future—

TALKING

Sometimes I wonder
    if people even need
    someone to talk to—
I think that if people
    would just shut their eyes
and start talking,
    talking just to talk,
to carry on a flow
    of just vocal thought,
then everyone could
    go home
and leave one
    just sitting, talking alone—

What's that?
    Wow! Wow!

That, my friends,
    is a poke
in your awareness—

No—just
    a duck splashing
on the marsh—

Man,
    in his good sense,
wrapped in his own
    good head,

talks to himself—

LONESOME

Have you ever been lonesome?
Have you ever been blue?

Have you ever been to Africa?
Well, so have I,
    let's screw!

(pause)   A Whazoo—

Have you ever been loaded,
brother, higher than a kite?
Start in smoking
   Monday morning
coming down on
   Sunday night?

Have you ever been a party
to a second hand rose?
Found her lover in the icebox
left him there,
   I guess he froze—

Have you ever been lonesome?
have you ever been blue?

DINING ROOM

Words
    an equation
        as in physics
a formula
  a vehicle
      to time & space—

You need not travel so great
a way as the world, nor so
great a moment as a lifetime
to perceive a universe—
if you could but slow down to
the natural rhythms of your
own being, then you could
experience a totality of time &
space that is the now, that is
happening in a presence of a room—

A poem must travel
    along lines of time & distance
much as a train must travel
    on its tracks
or as a circle must travel
    from its point—

A truth is subject
    to physical laws
as traveling is to
    time & space,
as the ocean is subject
    to motion & pattern,
        cycle & energy—

So is man, in thought
      & thinking,
    in past
    & present,
the flowing energy

that becomes
    the future—

So is man in thought
    & thinking
subject to its laws
    & its traveling,
as energy is
    in its passing—

The following is a statement,
    an expression
of my dining room:

    a small room
        with a large window,
access to three rooms
    by way
of doors & halls—

A universe
    formed by four corners
encompassed by boundaries
      of walls & floors
        & ceiling—

    A window & two doors,
to a separate but juxtaposed
    universe,
help define & negate its borders—

Sounds of Judy Collins
    with a memory-like sweetness
adds to this otherness—

A large window
    covered
      & complimented
by flowers & plants
    in glasses of water,
by burlap curtains

                    printed in flowers
                    of red & yellow,
                    of blue & more bright colors—

This dining room world
        becomes its own plant life,
green growth & motion
        that define
                        its own rigid form
                                of evolution,
each container
        a world
        of life seeking,
                supporting fluid,
penetrated
                by the roots
                        of seeking
                                & of substance—

Filtering through this water
                the light of the sun,
        so much
                the giver & partner
                of life,
taken once to be a god,
        now
                only a reflection
                        of his light—

Maybe it is the whiteness
                of the walls
        the basic color
                that is all color
that gives the time
                & depth
        to this room,
but there is a blending,
                a continuity
                        between what I see
        & what is beyond my sight
that makes the furnishings
                & furnished concepts

of all that is beyond—

The mirror in the hall,
    a dead-end of three walls
        into a corner,
that gives a glimpse to a room
        beyond my sight,
also gives a reflection
        of Winnie The Pooh,
    a water-color entrance
        to Tristessa's nursery
    & to Debbie in Ohio—

The walls, a mixture
    of art & colors
        given & created
of art
        lent or owned,
the feeling is one
        of nature & friendship,
    of wood & stone,
    of plant & flower
wedded
    with the paints
        & colors,
    the order
        & symmetry,
of myself & of friends—

There is a rug
    of antique
    & of oriental,
there is a dog
    of Australian shepherd
    & of hound,
both of history
    & of memory
    & of friendship—

Through this fixed world
    comes the changing
            & the constant
of family
    & of friends,
of music
    & mood & memory,
views of otherness—

A walk to another room
            & its return
    change completely
all that has gone before—

To make complete
    & concrete
is to include
    the change,
to make now
    was to add
            the will be—

Thank you for joining me
    in the now,
            in the was,
of my dining room—

            C.B. Luetkemeyer Jr.
            10.14.71, Monterey

FROM A CLASS PAPER, Monterey, 1971

A child is born as pure and empty as the sky must have been over L.A. a few hundred years ago. Not crystal clear blue skies, sunrises, sunsets, and that's all, but storms and wind also, a temperament, the beginnings of personality—

Blake's sense of religion, with its chapel of "thou shalt not", seems to me to be the smog that now fills the air over L.A.—religion has always been to me not a feeling of love, but of fear: love thy god or burn; love thy mother & father or you'll get your ass kicked & then burn—

I grew up in Catholic schools, grade school & high school, and learned nothing but what i could get away with, provided that I didn't feel guilty enough to tell on my self later—I learned that those in "black gowns" are like our boys in "green" gowns & "blue" gowns, with their codified systems of truth: all men are created equal, love thy brothers, peace unto all...except the blacks, the browns, the yellow, the white, the democrats, the communists, the heathens, the jews, the pagans, the etc...the excepts...

Priests in black gowns were walking their rounds,
cops in blue gowns were talking you down,
boys in green gowns were burning some town—

This poem brings many bitter memories, a very bitter response—

Love becomes an institution, as do all ideas that are followed instead of lived—the garden, maybe the garden of Eden, becomes a chapel, a church of salvation, a line of demarcation—

In a garden, flowers do not "die & are buried", but rather go back to the soil from which they came, in order that others may come after, nourished by the life that had been before—Blake, or I, sees that the very truth of our dying is denied—we are boxed up so that nothing benefits from our passing, except maybe the one who makes the tombstones—tombstones no doubt filled with flowery phrases, a block of granite with Love Forever written on it, but so cold to feel, so hard to the touch—

ANIMAL WALK

How does an
      animal walk?

Tension controlled
      relaxed
into
      fluid motion

that follows the
      contours of
         a hill

Garrapata flowing
      toward the
ocean below
      and a sunset

The hills tumbling
      beneath sage
falling over the
      weathered rock
to the sand
      & the sea below

VOICE OF THE SKY

What does the wind
    find to whisper about,
touching the very top
    of high ridge pines—

    The mute voice of the sky
& the clouds high above,
    white soundless tumbling clouds
pushing,
    blown along some
airstream boulevard—

Not the sound of rattling leaves
    but still articulate
in their very muteness,

piling three & four deep
    in the white granite gutters
of the high ridges,
    spilling over to
wash themselves down
    to form countless streamlets
& carry themselves to the sea
    far below—

Flowing, billowing clouds
    suddenly in spray,
        white & glistening
    in the sun,
exploding against
    some colossal boulder
in the bend of the stream—

Again follow
    the stormy, surging clouds
in the boiling storm,
        falling down
                the stepped contours
of the rocky gorge—

The blue sky,
        captured on the
                placid surface
of mirrored Meadow Lake;

        slowly diminishing,
                the meadow grows inward
on itself, forcing the
        water, clouds & sky
                down to the ocean
far below—

Peace, love, long hair & joints, San Diego, CA 1971

POEMS CRUMBLE

Don't try & humble me,
    motherfucker!

Your poems about
    green moss growing
            in gutters
as a garnish for godhead—
    I say fuck you
& your mellow presumptions!

That green grass grows
    regardless
of your abstractions
and even concrete breaks
    under the violence of time

                and crumbles back into the soil—

Luke, Chuck, Alex, Dianne, Gene, San Diego 1971

CLEAN & SILENT

The wave slaps upon the beach
 with a somersault & a slide,
it dashes across the rocks
 far back into the shadows,

and then it slips back again,
 a white foamy sound
that sets the rocks in movement
with a crash & a hollow thumping,

until finally, for just a tiny instant,
 it leaves the beach
  clean & silent,

 a space in which to write this poem—

ON HAVING A NICE DAY

Sometimes I feel so pressured
              into opening up
that I don't really
              want to have
                      a nice day—
     All the time
that the act of saying,
                      smiling,
     Good Morning
becomes in the acting
                      an act,
I feel,
     I mean
              I really feel,
that I'd like to tell
              an old lady,
              a pretty chick,
              a smiling hippy,
to take their
              Have A Nice Day
& shove it up
              their ass—

              Chuck, 9.27.71

A SNIPER PARANOIA

Hitchhiking,
picked up by paramedic,
    funky old car, Oregon plates,
gas & weed,
    paranoia after 2 tokes—

He's an ex-sniper,
    matter of fact
been shot 8 times,
    almost blown up—

All these stories
    and no emotion,
just more &
    more weed
and paranoia—

Did that black case
    really have medical books,
or one of those nifty
    breakdown rifles
w/sniper scope?

Home again,
    working on this
elaborate paranoia—

This guy was weird,
    he could be sitting up
        in a tree
staring at this window—

Have him busted,
    then he really goes crazy
        and six months later
            is now looking for me—

All scenes lead to that one fact—

RUNNING FROM THE GHOST

Moonlight Dancer,
    Necromancer,
what does your crystal show?

Wishing wells,
    and funeral bells
all laid out in a shining row.

It had something to do with the moon and the way you could draw your thumb across it, bringing a smear of light down to your eyes. Freezing light that numbs the gates of consciousness and frees the spirits from the dark places of your mind.

I was trying to read but was distracted by the shine of light staring across my shoulder. The moon was a haunting light, a guiding light beckoning to them, bringing them into the sanctuary of my now.

It was just a feeling, I told myself, just the end of a hassled day, too much uptightness, too many bullshit little things to stumble over from the morning until now. But still, I knew it was more than that, there was someone waiting beside me, something waiting for my fear to grow and acknowledge its presence.

With effort, I kept it outside of awareness and forced myself to get up and leave. I mumbled some sort of apology to Pam about flipping out as I put on my coat and gathered my books to leave. I could not have told her about what was waiting in the room, she acted so very normal, she would not have understood. Rather leave her wondering than to have to try and explain, it would only cause me to lose the hold that I had on my fear and be lost in it.

It hit me as I was walking down the street. In the house I could only feel the moon, catch an almost glimpse of it, knowing it was there but still be able to tell myself that it was nothing. But now, I had to walk with its light on my face. Its light too glaring to look blindly at my fear. The wind, once my only friend, just laughed and ran along the treetops, leaving me to walk alone with the ghosts that now crawled all through me, like termites in an abandoned house, eating through it so completely that its seemingly solid structure would crumble at the slightest push.

Only the habit of walking these same streets brought me home, I can remember only flashes of the way. I was lost inside myself, chasing after the ghost, trying to find out what it wanted from me or else running from the very secret I was seeking.

At times my running would bring me before the windows of my eyes and I would watch the people moving about on the streets. I was both amused and sad, and angry even, at the people who could move about so normally, pretending that they did not feel the ghosts that were walking among them. The laughing lights, the cars that stood mocking, deadly in their waiting, ghosts which could pass through their lives as the light of the moon passes over their faces. I wished that I could be like them, or at least that the knowing would be in them so that I would have someone else to share this fear with, not be so all alone in it.

It didn't seem right, that I should have this degree of consciousness in my dreams. I knew that I was dreaming, though I felt no different from when I was awake. The immediate past of the moment was that point in my room when I had sat down to rest from the flight through the moonlight. There was a slight difference, in that the surrounding streets and buildings would be familiar but for the feeling that I could not recognize where I was nor tell when I had last been there. I would recognize a street, only to have its name slip away from me because the houses that lined it should have been in a dozen different places, in a dozen other times.

I knew that the chase was to begin again now. The ghost of a moment ago came mocking, laughing, screaming at me. Only now it was more than a feeling of fear that I had to run from, it was a more physical thing. A dozen people emerged from the houses and began to run towards me, were running after me, as I was in flight long before I realized that the flight had once again begun. The chase had happened so many times that the physical motion of running, fighting, pain, were habits that only my body responded to, while part of me stayed in isolation, detached until some new variation was added to breach the walls of habit that were my defense.

My dreams. Here only was I familiar with the fear; I could not understand it, nor could I turn it away, but it had faces, names that I could use in spells of my own. I knew what gods to call, what places would be safe in hiding, just how far to run to calm my fears. I could even become the ghost and chase myself through the streets and buildings that were somehow familiar/confused. But it was almost the same as being chased, the fear

70

would not be gone, just replaced with hate; a feeling that was as poisonous in my system as the running.

There was only one place that was safe, that I could run to and not be followed. I could leave my dreams and pass once again into daylight. He would not follow there. After a few moments, I would even find forgetfulness and be happy with the sunlight. Then, even the ghost of the moon fading back into the night would be a part of the calmness that I moved in.

But if I was not caught and made to suffer for my running, I knew that I would have to run again, that the ghost was still inside, waiting as old friends wait across time to be together again.

But I am awake now, and the sun is shining. The wind comes again as my friend and now, leaving with him, I take a walk to the beach and enjoy this day.

Chuck 1.9.72

A ROACH

Through the focus of a grass high vision
      I try to formulate
a logical, verbal poetic
      about the roach
          lying unfinished on the table—

Through the added vision
      of a hassle-finished roach
I forget the poetics
      & commence to condemnations
          over grass distorted verbalizations—

By completing the circle
      to a stoned normalization,
I find that verbalizations,
      unfinished wanderings of poetics,
lead back to another joint—

                  Chuck, 1970 Something

I AM

I am what?
    I am nothing—

I am who?
    I am no one—

That is what?
    That is everything—

Who are they?
    They are everyone—

I react strongly to this—I fight it, I am above it, beyond it—

Who am I?
    I am everything—

What am I?
    I am everything—

Who are they?
    They are nothing—

That is what?
    That is nothing—

I react sadly to this—I am lonely—I am tired of my mountain, leave it to the Gods, their nature is more suited to its coldness—

I AM

Who am I?
    I am I—

What am I?
    I am I—

What is that?

That is that—

Who is that?
They are they—

I am more comfortable here, but I am too young to be this old—this wisdom,
this truth fits me like someone else's clothes, old man clothes from a bin at
the Goodwill—

Chaos is the birth of order
order dies into chaos—
flowers grow out of the earth
& die unto the earth—
Autumn into winter
Winter into spring
into summer into autumn—
cycles microcosmic into
cycles macrocosmic into
finite into infinity—
sadness into happiness
no lines crossed
just a cycle of attitudes—
nothing is any different
than anything else—

I AM

What am I?
(nothing)

What am I?
(   )

What am I?

Who am I?
I am they—

I am confused here, am mostly alone here, I am very different from them,
but I am no different than they—our lives are stories with different words,
are pictures shaded with different hues—one man walks on water, another

man splits the seas and walks through; all men drink of the water, all thirst without it, all men die without it—without water from the earth, men will dry up from within, just as they will flower with the water—I am a little less confused now; I am different, I am the same; just a matter of stories, just a matter of shading—

I AM

What am I?
    I am you—

Who are you?
    you are me—

You, me, we?
    I am—

Chuck 1.14.72

PASSING OF THE STREAM

Death,
　　our constant companion,
the only certainty
　　in a life of chaos—

No cruel master,
　　but rather,
　　　　or perhaps,
the answer to all questions—

Man in life,
　　like characters in plays,
wears many guises,
　　speaks endless dialogues,
leaving nothing settled,
　　nothing untouched—

Truth becomes filtered
　　like light passing
　　　　　through the silt of a muddied stream,
leaving half lights
　　& quarter truths
　　　　& finally nothing—

Death
　　walks by our side &
　　　　has nothing to say,
but this stillness & quiet
　　　　settles the mud
　　& the truth becomes clear—

It is just the passing
　　　　of the stream—

"While the rain washes
　　their faces
& cleans the salt of the tears
　　from their cheeks"—

Chuck 1.22.72

"I remember one day in St. Louis, Chuck gave me a homily on the mystical nature of nature as he saw it. He was standing under a tree. He picked up a rock and explained how it represented to him the image and presence of God. He explained that this point of view was his religion, and his understanding of God. I was surprised that he thought that way! I am so happy that he left those writings for you to put together as we all thought he had a lot of talent hidden somewhere. Ah, sweet mystery of life, eh?"

Sister Bede, Aunt

TIME TO A FLOWER

What is time
    to a flower?

It is
    the birth
        & the blooming
    the flower
        & the glory

It is
    the fading
        & the dying
    the seed
        & the renewal

of the flower
    & of time—

Without
    the death
        & decay
of time & space

there would be
    no bed for renewal
    no food for nourishment
no soil
    from which to spring
        or to return to—

SEVEN POEMS

CHAOS

Everything tries to complete itself—
all things fall into patterns, this is called order—
the opposite of this is called chaos—
chaos is the pattern of non-order—

□□□

REFLECTION

What do you see in a mirror?
What do you leave on that balancing point between reflection and reality?
Would you walk away and leave all of yourself which you reject,
taking that image which is an acceptable reflection back into
their reality?

□□□

LESS THAN ZERO

Is it possible for people to really make up anything that has no
basis in something that is real, something that exists outside of
a person's mind?

We see no real magic, no real ghosts—these are just phenomenon,
just mystery—

Are we progressing through science, or making things disappear?
Devolving by breaking down of the whole, subtracting from the whole
until we reach zero?

If the sum of the parts is greater than the whole, would not
the subtraction from the whole be even less than zero?

□□□

ART

Lines of dried blood
dividing his face
into sections—a piece of art!

□□□

CHOKING

If a person's self is kept
    within a set of boundaries
that are fixed and rigid
    he will stop experiencing
to keep from choking from within—

□□□

IS

When man is free
    from the bonds of technology
he will no longer be man,
    he will just be—
life without expectations,
    without planning,
becomes just a moment of
    is—

□□□

CRAZY

I think that I am crazy,
    but as long as I THINK THEREFORE,
I AM not worried—

Chuck 1972

UPON A BENCH

The Kiwanis club must have passed away;
    their name is now memorialized by
stone benches along the beach,
    set among the orange flowers
that line the path on the ocean—

I sat upon one bench
    as the evening was to begin,
  watching a seagull landing & marching
    upon a rock at the end of the path
like the Marine guard
    at the Arlington National Cemetery—

□□□

WINTER INTO SPRING

October
    with its passive days,
like old age
    sitting
on the late evening porch
    & awaiting death—

The passing of winter
    is attended by spring,
colors of flowers & green
    lay upon its grave;
the trees give voice to the wind
    the song made rich by the leaves

Chuck 1972

SITTING IN THE L.A. GREYHOUND BUS STATION
April fool day A.M.

A TV chair—"for viewing, <u>PLEASE</u>"—well, folks—I'm tired, in the early A.M. tired, been sitting on a bus all day tired, going to be on the bus 2 ½ more days tired, so fuck'em—the guy in the next seat, he has a pocketful of quarters, just settled down for a night of it—I can't see the screen, but it sounds like a German opera, maybe just a beer commercial—the TV has a small plate on it to let me know that it was made in Salt Lake City—if I was more into this tired state, I'd be into paranoid ravings about dark-faced Mormons making some kind of subtle pitch for my mind, but I don't anticipate that until tomorrow and by then they can have it—My Mind, brought to you by the Mormons & my mother—whee ha! Now the guy next to me has found some rock & roll, L.A. rock & roll, loud, electric, thousands of screaming young, young ladies throwing kisses & screams to a bunch of speed freaks humpin their guitars—screams & kisses, orgasms & cum, the whole scene about as sexual as an epileptic fit, sexual overkill—another tube behind me tells me about vitamins & extra energy—another has some really wicked laughter, dark, evil, oily Mexican laughter—talking about ugly orphans and "respected wishes of dead men…"

I wish they had a machine that would fly me to St. Louis for a quarter…of course, at only 20 minutes a 25-cent piece, I'd spend a fortune setting up residence—"Where you from?" "St. Louis, but I have a permanent L.A. address—if I ever stop putting quarters in my ear, it's back I go—cheap transportation, but really limited, huh?"

Well, that was a good twenty minutes, didn't cost me a thing, and while I'm still in L.A., I won't be much longer—

I got up this morning, picked up my income tax check, and ran away from home—funny thing is that I'm leaving home to go home—leaving that home that I fell into one day when I was down & out, living, 24 hr a day living, in a bar—Now I'm leaving all that I've known, loved, hated, clung to for a year & ½ to go "back home", that same home that I walked away from, in much the same manner I'm leaving this one; up & left years ago—leaving my mistress wife to take my wife as mistress—to be father to a little girl who is my daughter and an unknown person—a decision conceived in courage, an action finally through cowardice—good lord, confront me now!

I'm so down & lonely, that if someone walked up and touched me, or smiled, I'd probably cry—

"Been down, so down,
          the sky is probably grey
tho I haven't bothered to look"

If life were an ocean
     & I were a fish
     & god came passing over
          he'd probably pish

PORTRAIT OF an old woman sitting in the L.A. bus station—

Tiny black shoes, nothing fancy, plain sensible shoes, the kind of
shoes most old ladies in a bus station would wear—almost cheap, not quite
plastic, but not really leather...thin white cotton sox, all bunched around her
ankles, the tops just barely ending beneath a pair of very pale, bell-bottomed
slacks—not really belled pants, just wide, baggy pants, an ordinary white
blouse showing under a dark blue windbreaker—greying brown hair short &
tight over dark black frame glasses & a small pinched face—she returns
scowls for stares, a turned head in exchange for smiles—but then it's 2 am in
the L.A. bus station—I'm just a dirty, hairy hippie thing writing things about
her and staring at her ankles—small thin ankles, pinched like her face—
probably not made for walking, those ankles, even too thin to support her
socks, all bunched around the top of her shoes—I can't really imagine her
doing anything but sitting in this damn station—

Well, two hours down, two to go—if I can sleep, I'll wake up in
Arizona, just like Barry Goldwater—If I can't, I greet Arizona bleary-eyed,
bad-tempered, raving paranoid, just like lots of other folks sittin, waitin,
smokin cigarettes, walkin up & down, telling stories, swappin lies—I
thought I was going somewhere, feel like I never left—listening to the raps,
as I walk up & down smokin & waitin—"What do you think of L.A.
women?" a man, young boy, asks another—what women? Only ones I've
seen are just waitin & smokin—the ones I've seen aren't even here, just
somewhere between where they've been & where they're going—a lot like
most people, but it's easier to see that here—everyone here is relatin to the
same things, coming from here, going there, smokin & waitin—if I smoke
anymore, some dude is going to think that I'm just part of the pile of ashes &
butts and sweep me along with the pile accumulating in front of his
broom...Hell, sweep me up, I don't care, beats waitin, might even get
"there" sooner—Where am I going, anyhow? Oh, yeah, to St. Louis, says so
on this bus ticket stapled to my shirt pocket—"Send this boy to St. Louis,

easy on the starch"—bus tickets, laundry tickets, suicide notes, just going from there to there by way of here—

Wonder what Buttons is doing? crying, sleeping, bitchin at me, about me; just wondering, like me, what the fuck I'm doing—me, I'm sittin on the floor, lookin at shoes go by—lot of fancy shoes, but all male shoes—the women all have on old lady's shoes and don't walk much, just shuffle to a chair & sit down to wait—old scuffy flat black shoes that never go anywhere, just shuffle & sit down—unlike us men, us with our fancy shoes, our 50.00 hippie boots...all we do is walk around, then sit down, walk around—like the ladies, we're not going anywhere either, but we need these strong shiny shoes to walk around, makes us think we're going somewhere, or that we could go if we weren't already there, again & again already there—

All my heros are authors of books that I read to find out who I am, where I am—funny that I'm right here & all the authors are living the good life—Henry Miller wrote a book about Big Sur & his good life there—20 years later I'm running away from Big Sur & my good life there; he's down in L.A. now himself, only he's stayin & I'm just passin through—I'm out 2 bucks for his book, sitting on the floor in the L.A. bus station, & he's living in the hills, sleeping now, my money in his bank...I'd call him up to tell him so but he'd just want to know "So what?" & I don't know—

Or maybe I do—I just asked a chick, pretty & young thing, hippie-like, backpack, mountain shoes, I asked her "did she have the time?" She goes "Yeah, but not for you, Bro!" I mean, that's where I'm at—

TUES MORN
6 hrs in April Fools

EL INDIO—

We pull into this place in the pitch black early morning, this fool of a bus driver screaming 'bout breakfast—later the sun comes up, birds singing, we must be near some rail lines, every five minutes you hear this long drawn out lonely sound of a whistle, somewhere maybe in Arizona, telling all us folks at home that all's well, all's well—The sky is huge—I've been in the hills of Monterey too long, the contrast of the desert is most real—We should be going almost due east now, & for the next two days—tomorrow's sunrise is probably Texas, the day after, in St. Louis—Home!?!

THE FOOL'S DAY
32,000 Ft W. of St. Louis

Traffic problems over St. Louis, stacked (up like odds?) I doubt it—called Gene & Mike from Phoenix, no one home—all this was to go crazy in a bus station, plane depot, ridiculous—I'm so tired my head is fuzzy, I'm broke, I don't know where I'm going, but I sure know where I've been—wonder if I'm crazy enough just to push on—no, I'd end up in jail somewhere around Greenfield, Ill., busted while running amok in the town Laundromat, stark-naked, screaming about the greater & lesser Boohoos & all the other gods of a spaced-out trip—

PHOENIX
April Fools noon

30 Minute bus stop—decide I'll go slightly mad if I stay on this two more hours—a cash refund, a taxi ride, a very small but slow line at airport—some asshole ahead of me hasn't got the right papers to get into Mexico—he insists that he had straightened it out by phone days ago—the airlines officials are all smiles & "we understand, but..." The asshole, all he has to do is walk ½ a block, get a paper stamped & notarized, saying he was born, supposedly American-born, but any fool can see that he is both born & very characteristically American, but no, to prove he's American, or maybe even human, it's a common trait of man, he has to stand there & argue and threaten—the smiles on the faces of the ticket men are becoming more strained, frozen into place by training...just waiting for this to pass—When he finally gives way to the fact that he <u>can't</u> go unless he complies with the rules under which the system operates, one which he himself wanted, conceived and perpetuates, he stomps off leaving behind threats & accusations and relief on mine, and others, part—So I buy a ticket, get on a plane, drink a beer, eat a meal, land in St. Louis, take a cab to downtown, have Bro Mike pick me up, stay a night at his place, call Brother Gene, come to his place the next day, whereafter a day of "Blah-Blah" and bullshitting...I am sitting here trying to decide if I'm awake enough to go outside & take a walk; I know it's 30 degrees colder than I'm used to, but the sky is cloudless, the air crystalline, and the corn in the field, the mouse in the clock—As it is!

PART II

1973 – 1992

FROM A LONG NOTEBOOK ENTITLED: MEXICO, JUNE 73; YOSEMITE, JULY—AUG 73; ILLINOIS, SEPT—NOV 73

BUS RIDE TO MEXICO

California to Arizona to Mexico, bus riding all the way—really spacing out on the buses—wanted to do the strangest things; strangle some chick for playing her radio at 2 am—was in Guadalajara, hadn't slept in 2 days—here was this goddam music, I hate Spanish music, or at least the typical AM type radio Spanish music, like AM in states, pure bullshit, at 2 am, pure madness—listened to a couple of train engineers coming into LA early morning, really relaxing, country talking, slow, easy rap, not the words, just the music of such an easy flowing rap—wanted to shake their hands, or applaud, or laugh along with them—really appreciated the fact of just hearing them—

The Mexicans have a really crazy road system here, lots of stupid driving, lots of dead Mexicans resulting—the families place crosses on the side of the road to mourn their lost—passed a small stone, almost a miniature mausoleum, had flowers all over it, three votive candles inside—the saddest feeling came over me—this was about sunset, going through the mountains toward Salamanca & Mexico City—all jungle and long valley sweeping out down the mountains, ending on the horizon or just lost in the mist on the valley floor so far below—Some mother, maybe a thousand miles away on the border, maybe just twenty kilometers away in the jungle loses a son or daughter in an automobile accident, only the memory & the candle-lighting, the prayers to god to take their place—so what? I think everyone dies, everyone loses someone, whether to god, or to an automobile or a germ, so what—that's what was so sad—it means absolutely nothing; the earth claims its own, covers graves with green that soon dies & is replaced, green again—candles sputter & die, even marble crumbles, the earth slowly claims its own, god or not—so what?—So it is sad; that's all!

FROM A JOURNAL WITH POEMS
YOSEMITE, JULY—AUG 73

I am sitting on the Merced River, it runs the length of Yosemite—from here
I can see half dome on my left & Glacier Peak behind me—I was   not
impressed by much up until now, being too wrapped up by the bum vibes of
the crowds of campers around Yosemite Valley floor & by the hike up the
river to here, all brambles, mosquitoes & low hanging branches, an idiot's
trail, its only merit is that it follows the river & then much too closely for
decent walking—I would much prefer the high trails or the meadows up
around 6-7,000 feet—now though, now that I'm out of the underbrush sitting
on a gravel bar by the river, all surrounded by sunshine, gurgling, bubbling
river rapids, fallen logs, enormous cliffs of granite, I think that all before
was bullshit & that I'm only just seeing this place here—

□□□

> The walls of this valley
>   are so high,
> the sun leaves quickly—
>   Damn! I throw a rock
> at the advancing shadows—

□□□

> If the wind blew me off
>   this high peak
> only the clouds would know—

□□□

> The top of this peak
>   is eroded & pitted
> like the craters of the moon
>   through a child's telescope
> or the tide pools
>   when the sea pulls back

From here I can see the river winding thru Tuolumne over 2,000 feet below—Unicorn Peak sits to my back, only a few hundred feet higher than this rock I sit on—someone has taken an old gnarled stump and propped it here with rocks, I imagine it to take the place of a flag, the wind echoes the words "…in the name of the forest below, I name this peak…"—the wind forever blows away such flags & names—the stump will eventually rot, the richness of the wood will scatter to the floor below—the wind is the only thing that will remain here, the wind & the sun above—

□□□

Camping at Elizabeth Lake, Yosemite Peak, the lake is about 800 feet above Tuolumne Meadows and a 2 ½ mile hike up from the campgrounds below— the lake is very beautiful, rippled by the wind catching the last of the afternoon sun—a trout jumps, and the ripples expand in concentric circles, one is reminded of a spider's web catching the morning sun on countless drops of dew—

We have a camp on a large green meadow bordering the lake on the west end and nestled up to the walls of two peaks going up some 2,000 ft above— the sun us going down behind the highest of the peaks and already most of the cliff is in shadow, the shadows soon to cross the meadow, up through the forest east of here and up & over the mountains behind the trees—

We have a small fire and pot of vegetables boiling for the evening soup— meals have been mainly soups & peanut butter & jelly—not much weight, lots of energy & always a hungry feeling afterwards, not necessarily an uncomfortable feeling, but just a knowing-that-you're-there feeling—it really seems to sharpen my awareness of all that surrounds me—the meadow & lake are large enough so that darkness comes a couple of hours after the sun sets behind the mountain horizon leaving time to sit after supper, time to talk, maybe a game of chess, or just listening to the mountains relax and let night settle in—

□□□

A beautiful day, think that if I stayed here long enough, all my days would be fine—we broke camp this morning, the mosquitoes were so bad we had to eat in the tent and then we packed up in some kind of record time—Roger left us this morning to head back for Ohio and whatever trips he will get into there—a fine traveling companion, hope to hike some more with him one day—Deb and I have gone on, we plan to hike to Yosemite in three days, three very leisurely days—We are going to Cathedral High Sierra camp tonite, half dome tomorrow and then down to the valley following a side trip or two to the falls on Illouette Creek—We are taking a mid-day break now, beside a beautiful meadow right beneath Cathedral Pk—we are above 9,000 ft and keep coming through the forest onto views just incredible—we can see the valley floor at times & Tioga Rd. winding is way towards Nevada— We are now heading south and will be south & SW for the next 2-3 days—it is pleasant to look at the trail wind southward on the map—gives one the impression that the trip is all downhill—I cleaned up in the stream here—it collects in large rock basins, and the sun has warmed them enough to be quite comfortable—I wish the lakes were the same, but no, they are barely above freezing or so it seems—the meadow where we camped the last 2 days was covered with thick frost every morning and any water jug left out at night had a layer of ice on in the morn—the streams filter down from the peaks and quite a few seem to start under large drifts of snow & ice, still standing on the peaks above 9,000 ft—

□□□

The sky is a blue directly above me, this blue broken here & there by four or five huge white clouds, just a bit on the grayish side, possibly the forefront of the thundershowers that were occurring every afternoon for the last week and a half—the sky fades out as it nears the mountain horizon, the haze above the peaks blends imperceptibly into the washed out grayness of the rocks—As I look from the peak downwards I see dark patches here & there, stands of trees that somehow manage to grow above the tree line— then the true forest itself completely blanketing the lower slopes of granite— There is a beautiful lake below me, blues fading into green, and then the yellow-brown of the sandy beach--Coming up from the lake is a small stream—where it empties into the lake, it is just a weaving blue line, but as I follow its trail backwards thru the meadow, I can see the green & brown moss growing on the rocks in the stream, the tops showing white from the many washings of melted winter snows—the meadow is a rich dark green, interspersed with red flowers, and a few yellow & purple, though these are very few & take a bit of looking to pick out—the red ones grow in large patches and with the green remind me of Christmas wreathes—Behind me are cliffs of crumbling rock, more like huge gravel pits, though they go up over 1500 ft—I followed a creek up to the snow drifts that feed into it, and

beyond picking my way up the rocks, some bigger than my house in P.G.—
some are huge slabs, four ft thick and easily 200 sq yds of surface area—the
rocks seem to just flake off in huge sections and slide down the slopes,
leaving a trail of sharp fragments behind them—from the top I could see that
there were three lakes below instead of one; the largest, Young's Lake,
which Deb & I are camping at—the other two are unnamed, and unshown on
the map—I believe I'll call them Linda's Lake & Trissy's Lake—The lakes
are terraced one above the other and feed into each other by streams winding
down thru the trees & rocks—Between the highest & the middle lake is a
waterfall, dropping about 15 ft into the creek pools below—I thought of
calling this Love Falls, and making a poem out of it, but, maybe later—

□□□

What a fine way to spend the day—I got up this morning, the sun had been
up for a couple of hours, but we are camped on the east side of the lake and
because of the peaks behind us & the trees around us, we don't get direct sun
for a few hours after it comes up—We had a fine breakfast of French toast &
hot chocolate, and some beans left over from yesterday—After cleaning up
the camp, dishes, bodies & the general area, we both decided to take off for
the day—Deb wanted to go down to a meadow below & watch the
animals—she is doing studies & drawings of the area—I thought I would
hike down to Tuolumne & get some wine for the evening—it was a very
pleasing walk—I was alone all the way & could stop & dig on things as I
felt—I saw two really beautiful meadows—the first was a place that I would
probably be satisfied to live in for the rest of my life—I had a whole fantasy
trip on what I would be like and had to make an effort to dispel these
daydreams & get on my way again—The second was nothing special, except
for the stream running across it & three deer feeding on the greenest grass I
have ever seen, just unbelievably peaceful—

□□□

Now I am sitting on the edge of the parking lot by the Tuolumne Meadows
store, digging on the people coming & going, also getting into my third beer,
first beers in four days, & I really can get off on the taste—the slight high—I
can really enjoy the mountains here, I feel more at ease than I have been
doing just about anything, but it is just fine to sit back with a can of beer and
dig on that which is going on around me—It is like a time-out from living,
the only awareness is one that you make yourself, or at least edit at your

89

leisure—though I know that the hike back to camp, with the slight head I've gotten, will probably kick my ass—the trip is only 7 miles or so, but half of it up hill, a gain of 1200 ft, to about 9,800 ft—the air here was made for goats & eagles, not beer drinking people—but then again, that comes later & now the beer is just fine—

□□□

And now the mood is color—I sat & watched the sun go down—The cliffs behind turned orange, the snow had streaks of red thru them, the drifts that stay this late into summer undoubtedly pick up traces of the rocks, and they are made up in part by a reddish-brown stone quite different in texture & color than the (marble-granite) that is the dominant stone here—just as the sun goes down over the western slopes, the moon comes up over the opposite peaks, following the sun forever on a merry chase around the earth—Tonight it was not quite full, but seemed enormous, slightly orange upon its ascent above the cliffs, soon brilliant white, casting long shadows off the trees, leaving its reflection dancing on the rippled waters of the lake—

□□□

NIGHT IS A DOORWAY

Night is always present,
it does not fall
  as the sun sets,
nor does it steal in
  to claim the earth
like a thief coming in
  the back door
    after the master leaves
(No,
  I think that it is present
    always, thru day & night,
  this blackness)—
Night is a doorway,
  an entrance to the mind,
to the deep caverns of ones self—

It is here,
      hidden away from light,
that things & creatures
      stir & slither, slimey
crawling wet things,
      cold to the touch,
all that is evil & repelling—

             □□□

VISION OF THE STARS

The fire this cold night
      gives me a small circle
           of warmth,
this I feel,
      hot on my face,
holding the cold on my back
      at a comfortable level—

The light is thrown
      further than the warmth;
giving comfort also, it holds at bay
      creatures of the night,
those that walk on four feet,
      on two feet,
those that crawl on bare earth
      & somehow those
that crawl & walk
      inside the darkness of my mind—

Small this comfort,
      for it blocks the vision of the stars;
the hissing & popping of the fire
      hides the singing, whispering of the forest—

A WAY TO BE WALKED

Life is like traveling in the woods,
it can be easy or it can
be difficult—
there is a feel to the
land, it has a way to be
walked, it lets you know
how to get around (how difficult is the going?
is it smooth, comfortable
walking ? let it just flow, find the rhythm)

Would a person travel
a path that was strewn with
fallen logs, patches of mud,
straight through brambles,
thorns, when there was a meadow
nearby, all green grass
& scattered white rocks?

HIGH PASSAGE

Whispers of wind
　　that touch at the tops
　　　　of mountain pines

the faintest of sounds
　　I'm not sure of hearing
　　　　their high passage—

Sitting now
　　high above the pines
the wind that whispered below
　　roars now across barren rock
the air is thinner here
　　only the sun
& a few distant peaks
　　can hear this sound

But the peaks
　　are still numb with snow
and the sun is forever in a vacuum

EARLY MORNING RADIO

Ho! I spin the dial
    on this early morning radio
& hear mountain streams
    dancing across
white polished stone—

counterpoint to old Dylan chords
    & the bitter sweet sounds
of love lost & gone,
    as brief as
telegraphs
    & haiku,
they twist among the strands
    of smoke
rising from a number—

    suddenly frozen
like a stream dying & held
    ice-bound in cascades of winter
or an eagle, wings spread,
    suspended eternally
against pure mountain sky—

    another instant
and the image of an eagle
    slips into a sliding glide,
while below
    the streams dissolve
into a slow motion flowing
    across the face
of white polished granite—

all of these strands
    loosely woven
into the fibre of a song
    draped over the shoulders
of an early morning sleepless high—

(Dylan's harmonica,
    Jack Eliot's rambling—
funky mountain mama
    rocking away the early evening—
the light fading as quietly
    yet as clear as memory)

BULLSHIT

Bullshit bullshit bullshit bullshit
bullshit bullshit bullshit bullshit
bullshit bullshit bullshit bullshitttttttt

And so, things swing in a full
circle—from town to another
country, to town from another
country—I leave, only to return,
the city drives me to leave,
the country drives me to return—

I read maybe too much from
what happens around me—
I see that all that happens
is just the surface of things,
the light that reflects off
of the river is just a part
of what is happening—

What?? Bullshit? No,
not even that—just words—

I miss, long for, the smell
        of the woods,
the thump-thump beating
        of my heart
the climb to the tops of peaks
        makes me real,
my heart thumps, tries to leave
        my chest—

TOWN & COUNTRY

A blank page,
    like empty days,
stares back at me—
questions of filling
feelings of doing
restlessness in place of resting—

Town fills me with boredom,
    energy unused,
energy to use,
    things to do, places to go,
these are all illusions
    that vanish with distance,
the Country, the woods
    settle these feelings
like silt traveling a river—

A FACE IN THE DARK

Lives,
    cars passing in the night,
giving glimpses of those inside—

We see but a face
    and build whole persons,
lives that touch on parts of ours—

A face in the dark,
    memories & dreams at night,
only hint at lives as they pass—

Is it dawn & its bright light
    that push back the shadow
and reveal only lives & their passing?

Memories, dreams, glimpses of past
    give way to the first rays of morning,
are left behind with the darkness of night—

Chuck 1973

I have rapped with a few people lately. I mean that I've rapped with a few people & the rap is just basically the same—they are alone, feel alone, are hemmed in by thoughts unspoken, held in tight restraint, or maybe just dribbled away in rumor-type release—just bare hints of problems, no real communication, just the aftermath of bad feeling expressed in tight shoulders, curt, terse words, silences as heavy and as meaningful as a half a day of awkward rapping: "Baby, I'm so uptight, don't know what's coming down, but I've got to rap with you—something, black & heavy as a sudden summer storm is building in my head—I don't know just why, but if I can't find to rap it out, I'm going to blow it—I love you Babe, but I can't talk to you & get across what I'm feeling & I feel I must, I have to, I see just bad vibes & downhill feelings from here—I love you Babe, we were so innocently happy, that nothing blew the slightest, coolest shadow on the childlike sunshine, that seeming forever sunshine of late spring & early summer."

FROM A JOURNAL ENTITLED: Leaving Anacortes & Secret Harbor
Cohasset bound
Calif trapped
again 7.18.74

We sold the van to Butch, rented a U-haul truck & finally got out of Dodge, Anacortes—we spent 2 nights sleeping on 18th st. in the trailer, walk a ½ block to the ABC body detailing & towing to use the john—We do this, we do that and some more of this & that—we cash out $3,600 or so—

FOOLS

So, aren't we all fools then,
    wanting to take a walk
just to see the leaves fall,
    floating down on an evening breeze?

The papers tonite shouting at me,
    telling of people dying,
            people dying,
of hitchhikers slain, troops deployed,
    governments apologizing, threatening
ultimatums and restitution—

Maybe we are all fools, then,
    to take a hot bath
and write a letter to a friend
    about the mellow feelings of a wine high?

So sad to take a walk
    & see a child beaten
    in anger,
a dog kicked, a friend put down,
    people passing, heads down, strangers,
feelings unshown for fear of laughter—

Is it so wrong to be a fool then,
    to write a poem to a friend
& be selfish enough to say hi,
    & think only of myself & you?

                    Chuck 3.11.73

ALONE

One of the moods of today,
    I mean maybe
a national mood,
    is one of loneliness—
the feeling that one is the
    center of the universe
that all events
    all peoples, cause & effect
    stem from our own
thoughts & actions—

Still we touch
    each other
        now & then
that we can be
    a part of each other—

But still again
    the feeling comes
that we are totally alone
    nothing between us
but the lines we draw
    around ourselves
        and one another
(a vacuum surrounding us
    that the sounds of voice
    can't ever penetrate,
that the warmth of feeling
    might never cross—)

The illusion of smiles,
    like the glow of the sun,
seems to cross this space
    that seems not to exist
but this warmth holds
    only a remembrance of feeling
not quite the flush
    of an evening of wine—

Elsah, Illinois, Summer 1975

It was 1975. I was living in an isolated house on a hill on 80 wooded acres outside the little Christian Science town of Elsah, Illinois, on a bluff above the Mississippi River. Chuck had come in from Pacific Grove, CA, to hang out and had brought with him a penchant for junk and his own personal rig, the needle and glass tube of a syringe attached to a rubber squeeze bulb that he'd assembled himself. It was a gnarly affair. There were always new, antiseptic outfits around, but Chuck believed in the mojo of objects, and he was attached to his makeshift rig. There was a proliferation of Mexican Brown heroin in those days, dark, dirty and unpredictable, and soon Chuck's rig was put to use.

There were other guests at the Elsah house at that time, a shadowy gathering of miscreants and malefactors, one such being David, a federal fugitive laying low while he pondered his next move. David had been a medic in Vietnam. One day he came to me and said I should keep an eye on Chuck, that he might be getting a little reckless with the Mexican brown, that in fact, the previous night, while I was out somewhere, he'd come upon Chuck sitting motionless in a chair in the dark. He'd tried to rouse him but couldn't, so he gave him mouth to mouth resuscitation and put him under a

102

cold shower. I waited a couple of days before I related this to Chuck, not wanting to embarrass him. He listened and nodded and said, "Well, funny, last night I came into the living room and you were lying on the couch and I said something and you didn't respond and I came over and shook you and you were cold and blue. I gave you mouth to mouth and slapped you till you came around and kept you up till I was sure you were ok."

I think if I had not mentioned his episode to him, he would not have mentioned mine to me, not wanting to embarrass his host.

Gene

I remember other small things about Chuck. I remember when I went to visit him in Monterey and Pacific Grove. It was snowing in Monterey, something it doesn't do much there. Even Chuck was surprised. Most times we were getting stoned. It was the first time I had seen Chuck shoot heroine. Many of my memories are foggy due to too much drug taking of my own.

Luke

JUNK

There is a weightless feeling
on junk—not a rising above
it all freedom, but a freedom
of slashed moorings, of a
drifting from the light of day—
not the screaming, desperate
fall from the edge of sanity,
but a slow motion falling
through the dark vacuum of
someone else's mind—

In the beginning was junk,
   & junk was the beginning
    & the end—

     Chuck
     10.28.71

$14.95

A NOVEL

By Chuck Luetkemeyer

"What the fuck is to say," he said, "I mean goddamn it, what the fuck is to say?" The words as unheard as lyrics to a song played on a radio listened to by one deep in thought, the music no more noise than the sounds of the freeway passing over the rooms of a house subdivided by the Cal Trans Authority & State Highway 99.

"I mean, goddamn it, have you ever heard, or rather not heard, the words of some juke box honky-tonk love song played so many times an hour every fuckin day of the week, day after goddamn day for Christ knows how long?"

The bar was closing down for the night (day maybe, it was almost dawn). Good time Charlie & G.I. Bill were holding down the end of the bar nearest to the john, listening to Zach the Barkeep bullshit & pontificate with about as much attention as they give the jukebox; giving them credit for the fact that they played almost all the songs over any given evening. "Any kind of music will fill up the void, those spaces between here & there—those kinds of music picked as totems to ones own personal mojo & style unconsciously and ritualistically give the hearer (non-hearer) control over the ticking that fill out the mattress of life, squirmy crawly smelly bed of creation, but not a bug or spring that is not accepted as essential to life & a good night's sleep."

"All this and probably more, heard or not heard by G.I. Bill," thought Good Time Charlie, "This dude is probably short circuiting again listening to this barkeep."

For himself, Good Time Charlie was paying more attention to the door to the john, wondering if the chick was going to connect the charcoal smudge on top of the toilet tank with the cotton floating in the bowl with the cool son of a bitch at the end of the bar; wondering if that foxy hunk of fluff would equate such an open, macho, bravo existential act of outlawed self-destruction with the heavy looking, quiet dude at the end of the bar; kind of bored, waiting politely for a break in the hour-long monologue that was, is, forthcoming from the barkeep.

"I mean, I spend so much time, time that is a one-time thing, behind this bar, that I become too conscious of, too sensitive to, the noise that is silence; the silences that are the true noises, the grunts and moans, sighs and whys, audio and visual phenomenon that make up and interact the dialogues and monologues that make up this reality of what I speak, of the unspoken that I have heard...I spend so much time concerned, nay, obsessed with these meta-auditory perceptions that I cannot continue to function as a mere barkeep, content in a $3.35 an hour social role of servicer to ones in need of service," said Zach, the barkeep, knowing that his rap, and it was a rap, was only partly wasted on the post-grad doctorate type fem that was staring deep into his eyes; mirror-like she gazed into his eyes, rather, the reflection of his eyes; mirror-like she gazed deep into her own abstractedness, marveling at the depth of her understanding and at stranger's knowledge. Not since that dark one, Professor of Blackness, had she been so entrapped by the gravity of her own soul; felt the weight of her own existence touch other than vacuum. "It is so true," she echoed in her thoughts, "this man knows the sounds of silence, the non-sounds that register such vibratory orations on the metaphysical membranes, such throbbing on the primeval drums that stand between the physical and the perceptual."

As these abstract auditions echoed off the wall of her soul, they struck disharmony with the bestial braying from the end of the bar—the G.I.'d, O.D'd. scraggly haired, half bearded one that was called G.I. Bill, calling, demanding, "More beer, barkeep, more beer!"

Zach was there before he finished speaking, grabbing the empty and placing another within reach, though far enough away so not to be upset, overturned by the manual gyrations that accompanied over the simplest vocalizations of this one who used to be an ex-Vietnam vet.

"Another beer, barkeep, and more of the same; I mean, your rap, your ramblings & ravings," said G.I. Bill, eyes focused tightly on the gregarious Aquarius of a barkeeper, "such a verbiage of words, if you can't dazzle 'em with brilliance, baffle 'em with bullshit—another beer for this one here, too. 'ol Charlie will probably throw it up, but enough B vitamins probably be absorbed and sugar sucked up for nourishment that is more holistic than not."

Zach nodded, popped another top and slid it across to the quiet one at the end of the bar who looked over, nodded in turn and went back to his waiting, wondering—

"What if this fine piece of fluff was hitting up herself, though her arms were clean as statues of the Madonna, as clean as an infants' perception of a grandmother, maybe she pulled her skirt up around her waist, sweaty fingers probing deep into fleshy thighs, feeling for that pulse of life artery, sliding a sharp new point down towards the bone, waiting for the jet of blood to register, slowly pressuring the junk into the dark tide, halfway booting the junk and blood back into the fit, watching it mushrooming for a second, then a final squeeze, pulling the point out ahead of the red ball of blood that runs down the side of her thigh, unnoticed as the rush grabs her by the back of her neck, needles and pins, fire pricking her shoulders—her eyes and sinuses watering, throat closing off, gag reflex, the smell of sulphur jolting his dormant olfactory centers, Good Time Charlie wonders again, "Am I some kind of psychic, is this chick really into morphine or am I just deluded again, remembering those shrinks in Bezerkely, trying to explain those dream excursions through the nether regions, old Black Professor I.M. Morpheus, astral guide and defrocked metaphysician, leading the way through the various rings and phenomenon, his dark acid words falling on his head, shoulders, a preview of those rushes that were the only thing he could remember out of all those weeks spent in the recovery ward before returning to the world—that second to the last acid trip that told him he would die one day, though not this time, not in this tangle of twisted metal that had been someone's own private and personal space a moment before.

he had been trying to explain the old Mad Morpheus dreams, the ones that this acid trip had shown him to be more than psychic, not only would these dreams show to be portents of rushes and vibes to come, they would show that what would be, was already, and would always be happening—past, present and future be godamned!" said Charlie, shouting over the music, static mostly in the growing storm. He shifted sidewise in the front seat, looking over at the lady driving him home. "All that is now, is now, is, was and will be are all the very same thing. Oh, wow, what the hell am I babbling about? It only makes sense if you don't try to talk about it—do you know what I mean?"

She looked over at him smiling, as if to say "I can dig it; even if I don't have the slightest idea of what you, my fine old flaky friend, are trying to say, I can dig it."

NOTHING TO TELL

I think that it is important
to remember everything that
is happening around me, all
the sounds & sights, the
smell & feelings, all
the vibrations of a room, a
house, a crowd of friends—

for god is not one of us
& cannot know as we know
and when I die & stand before
him, he will ask me all that
I have seen or heard, so that
he might be a part of it—

the pain of it all will come
from experiencing the sadness
of god if we have nothing
to tell him—

Aug 5.75

AND SO! We have a beginning, with just a couple of words; two words, one step towards seeing where I'm bound, from seeing where I've been—a good day to begin—money situation is just fine—tomorrow pay Gene, buy a car, fuel the living situation, and the stash is still just left with enough coins to seed another crop—moving towards? Pfalzgraff Ceramics, place to live up near here, country, pot & pottery? Illinois? Fall! No matter where! My mental energy is quite high, a brain with thoughts, plans, commitment, but my gitup is still waiting to get up & go—but yet, find that I'm definitely moving towards a more peaceful ground, a fine time for growing— Physically I'm becoming quite healthy, no tiredness, energy returning to point of restlessness, boredom to ripen soon, energy released something to forming—looking back, a long road, but less and less stumbling, surer of foot, learning to think, plan again—trying to realize some kind of subtle, unconscious plan of 5-6 years (28 yrs?), brewing time is now! Back on the merry-go-round—another empty space to fill; pages to fill, junkyards to gather, others to clutter—definite forms appearing from scattered & regathered energy—stay high, but stay straight—lot coming up, keep in touch—

1975

Old Man Winter, taking the guise of grey skies & cold, leaf-filled winds, comes at a rush; and all those spring days lie heaped in a pile of Indian Summer illusion, like the leaves wind-heaped against the cold brick walls of this house—from one page to another, one day to another, a different place, continued…

Illinois—mid fall, grey days, cold, sudden wind, leaves rushing back to the warm womb of earth, creating future life from their embrace—

Life's scenario—working, cooking, trade my time for a few coins & doggie bags—'49 Chevy, being re-built, mechanical metamorphosis, its own fall rites—

FROM A 1976 POCKET CALENDAR

JANUARY

Fight w/Buttons • Nothing—fuck—broke again—will I ever learn? Doubt it!
Woke up sick—Catch up on letters & papers—Buttons back wens • Woke
up still sick—ltr to V.A.—hocked rifle for 15.00—ltr from mom • 104.00
Gene—almost well • Hauling job • Clean Randy's house • LOST
SOMEWHERE • Went to Whiskeytown • Camping • Get-it-together-day,
need money • NOTHING • NOTHING

FEBRUARY

Grass Valley—Nevada City, need to move • A cold wet day, 1st in weeks •
Ltr from Michele • Hock rod & reel 10.00, pd Steve • 125.00 from Squeak—
Buster coming up—Steve 5.00 IOU • Gun hock due—pd interest another
30d • Yuba City Doldrums • Wasted City Blues • Owe Squeak 35.00—owe
Anthony 25.00 • Sold watch & purses 35.00 • Package to Tris, Bday—cards
to Linda, Debbie—Sold chair, Ivory, basket, pitcher, ring—50.00 •
Kickback day—paid Rick 5.00, pd Squeak 10.00, pd rent

MARCH

To Monterey—Barb's place overnite—5.00 from Rick—gas 7.00 •
Monterey—saw Michele, Clancy, Diane, James, everybody, bummed out
trip so far, a total loss, motel 14.00, Buttons 10.00 • Tris Bday—beautiful
day—Big Sur Party Time—Fred, Denise & Steve • Jade Cove, back to Yuba,
Dinner at Steve's, Kathy, Nile—Cork turned me on • Long walk on Feather
River—ltr frm Debbie Fox—Buttons home • Michel B.D., Ernie & Paula
M.J. bust ticket, Squeak got her house, Steve busted, Dido to pound, Gary
moved in w/Penny • Nothing happening so far—Anthony by, Squeak to
hospital—vibes unbelievably down & out—people the most flipped out I've
seen yet • Steve to SF, Diane due again, Rick OD'd, Anthony busted, IRS
42.50, Rick out of hospital, Indian curry supper, told Squeak to fuck off •
Buttons down to Ventana, talking moving, almost full moon, Katie math & a
hug, rapped w/Ernie & Cork till 4 am • buy food stamps, pkg to Tris, a
nothing day—too many people—hanging out—Buttons back thurs—full
moon madness vibes • touch of hep still, hard to wake up, talked to Buttons,
back tomorrow pm, profitable; money vibes, connections • wasted day—
Buttons called, car fucked in San Jose, Randy went to hospital, packed

everything to lv—Kate & Cork to go to Ariz in am • Katie & cork off, Pattie kicked out of house, Randy ok but what an ass—Buttons back, up till late packing—getting out of here • moved out, what a fuckin hassle/relief, spaghetti dinner, Squeak w/David—no sleep until Mon am • go down the coast, stopped in S.J. to see Rose, country bar & beer, first good sleep in days • reading & the dogs—Pfieffer Beach, nice sunny day—kicked back at Fred's, sun, dogs smoking & reading, mellow days so far, crashed & good nite • Up at Michele's, not much happening, Buttons & Michele rummage sale—packed the car & down to Big Sur • Lazy day, checked out Ventana campground, went up and talked to Charles & Dick—job on trial basis, keep it straight, work like hell—start sat., not much else • Went to Clancy's, steak & wine in front of fireplace—good nite's sleep & woke up feeling good—

APRIL

In town, Michele's, packed car, down the coast again, moved into tent, nice feeling—cold & damp but think that will change • Worked—really a hustle, change, but I think it will mellow out—food is good; walked up this canyon—logging • Worked evening w/Charlie—up till 2:00 am, rapping deals, swapping highs—walked up canyon, checked camps, trails, future hikes—stayed w/Charlie • Up late, to Ace's for beer & spaghetti, saw Corky at hot dog stand • up late, foggy headed, breakfast at Michele's, back to Ventana, kind of a sunny day, moved tent up the canyon • For a month it looks up at Charlie's, going to work, work a bit of a hassle but—cocaine, weed, poker w/Steve, Charlie & Buttons—real mellow • Clancy down, mellow nite but a drunk one—gallon of red • Up the hill, sitting in the sun, supper, couple of doobs, reading & good nite • up early, went into town but didn't stay—Mike called, my dad died thurs nite—passing of the seasons, born in the spring, it took him back in spring—passing on through • Run around, cashed Alan's chk, off to St. Louis—plane flight was really spaced • Met Mike & Alan, back to Cahokia, then to Freeburg w/mom, Sandy, Debbie & Dave—met all of family—dad looked like himself • Funeral, 1st sunny day for a while—rapped with family, dinner afterwards—Pat came in from PA., back mid-afternoon—drinking lot of beer—feeling sad, but mellowly high • Just hung around—went to Georgia's, picked up dad's car & belongings—up to Elsah, Gene's—no one home, picked up a couple downers & home—wasted night—Buttons called • Visit, sit around, get high, rap, get money together to fly home—everything over but the leaving • Plane day, St. Louis to Phoenix to SF to Monterey, Buttons picked me up, down at Diane's, back to Big Sur—saw Charlie—home, screwed, lewd & nude •

MAY

Buttons picks me up at work, home, laze around, go to work, beers at the bar, foggy, worked dinner, steady mellow nite, home, crash out, smoke dope • Pfieffer Beach, coral shells, hang out in tent, buy bottle of vino • Breakfast w/Buttons, down to Little Sur, really nice abalone, screw, shower, work, get high, home again, Buttons home—rap & laugh • Slow day, borrowed 3.66 from Terry—bottle of wine & smoking & reading—Buttons home w/weed—half drunk, but wired until early morning • Ran into Rodney & got some dope—down the coast, mellow—took a shower & kicked back • Buttons & I up to Diane/Dennis & Dave—back down, party was fucked—Charlie's—from Pismo, Martin & Pam (sing), Rick space/basket case, Shana & Robin (nice teeth), cocaine, weed & beer—weird thing with camera & pies…crash heavy, but…• Whole day wasted coming down from nite before • Cut tree to make post & pad to punch/kick • Moved the tent, got laid, stoned, had bacon & eggs for breakfast—real mellow for a change, actually feeling better • Hung over, but the spirit if not the flesh revived—need to curb some piggy impulses, going to nowhere but trouble • Smoked, laid, read, River Inn for spaghetti & beer—Pfieffer Canyon, smoke, rap crash • Just a day, tired of working, saw Taxi Driver, Sean back to Sur • Slow day—read, screw, eat, sun, good vibes, slow—time to relax • Clancy & Michele to Kalisa's, belly dancing, home again, crash too late, no sleep, back to work • Cork & Kate back from Ariz, River Inn with Buttons/Kevin—weird place • food, beer, jukebox—Clancy decided to go to Yuba City to get it together again—all start, no finish

JUNE

Move into Steve's, nasty day, life's a grind, work a drag, Steve leaves a mess • An all day grind, too much of a hassle • Steve gone, people coming in, really nutty, a taste of the summer—smoking at work is a bummer • Too much noise—everyone sulking—why is what I say or do so important to people—what a waste of time & space energy—work all day, to come back, get stoned & wish I wasn't—too much confusion—bullshit • New chef/consultant—change coming at Ventana, vibes weird, weed makes zombies of us all—all is trips—see things that oughtn't be there—home, mellow, wonder, crash • Things at work always confused as of late, too much bullshit, slow, called back into work to lite an oven, what a bunch of turkeys—not much happening—just can't seem to make anything come together • Walked out, just couldn't handle it anymore, Buttons not at all surprised—maybe a hippie again—Katie, Sean, Lisa, Jenny down south, camp at Naciamento, Fernwood, Mexican food, beer—quiet night, resting • Up early—feeling guilty about work but getting over it rapidly—Alan & I took a long & high walk—what a view • Talking a trip, Ariz & Sierras—Buttons, Alan to Mont—me? just read, lay around to relax, be mellow again—just smoke, relax—nothing—talk more of going somewhere • Eggs for breakfast—Alan & I to Molera, long hot walk—Buttons quiet, just packing & waiting • Monterey—camp in VFW Park, bought Dodge Dart 225.00, split for Y.C. • Car died—75.00 to fix timing chain, 50.00 for tires, 15.00 for distrib • Sell Dart 500.00 for 135.00 profit, '48 Chrysler Windsor for 300.00 • Cooling system fucked up—50.00, trade for '66 Ford truck—Y.C. sucks as ever • Saw Steve & Rocky, Chuck & Ernie—nothing new, everyone mellow • Clancy turning into some kinda old lady/cheap shot • Corky had job, lost job—went on binge, lost money—really—

JULY

Mellow otherwise—now job/house in Chico (1 July 76), Clancy maybe to Ariz • Alan & Squeak sleeping together, Buttons on welfare, middle July • Camp at Feather River Canyon, stop Oroville—to Caribou Canyon at dark, tent up & kick back time, good night's sleep, cool • To Quincy for food—real nice drive, the town is in a huge valley surrounded by mts & firs—moved from Caribou to Holsted, right on the Feather river—spent the day swimming, beer & goofing—fire later in evening—cold nite sleep • Buttons into Y.C. for welfare—Alan & I went up river, swim, hike & beer—laze around, Buttons back with Squeak, another tent, food, beer, a lid—had a nice fire • Camping, swimming, sulphur baths, drunk, good times • Played pool, breakfast in Quincy, just mellow time—lid of weed, no good but quite a few turn ons—no real bad vibes, nice to be mellow so many days in a row—back to Y.C. • Corky to Chico, move in, work as R.N. here in town—Squeak trying to get out of Air Force • Clancy & Asa to Ariz • Paid 200.00 to move in Chico, 67.50 cleaning deposit, not bad apt—went to see Jaws—back home, smoke & fire • Just hanging out—Y.C. blues—Alan & Squeak trip well together—two Gemini's, right! • Buttons & I take load up to Chico...smoke some good weed, back to Y.C., nothing happening, there never is • set up most of house—the vibes feel good here, thinking about what to do—school, pottery, karate • Garage sailing—feeling sick—just hung out, tried to pretend I felt fine; not much on fantasy, felt bed, bed early • Swim at Bidwell Park, shopping & house trip • Swimming at Maffalia, talk w/Rob—what a turkey—got high, just kicked back • Cork & Kate • Buttons to Mont, take smoke to Fat Cat • Saw Michele, Kyia, Sean, Kevin—Michele kinda frazzled, wants to go anywhere—Corky called in sick • Up early, sell 49 Chevy for 50.00—pick up our stuff, stop in S.J., Campbell, pick up Buttons' transcripts • Oroville for food stamps (70.00) Squeak & Alan down, out of USAF—going So. Cal, then Ariz, then Ill. • Wine high—Corky quit job—

AUGUST

Buttons accepted at Chico, Rob gone, hurrah • Camping, Lassen, Redding— 13 hours of driving, pizza in Redding & came home at 1 am thurs—a real weird trip—karma, neh? • Space day, not much happening, not much happening • Corky's Bday, up at 4 to go fishing, N. Fork Feather, no fish, but a fine breakfast—up to Butte Lake to camp & fish; no fish but a fine camp w/wine • Corky off to Ariz, but truck in Y.C. break down—back on bike • Buttons, Cork, Kate off to Ariz, last minute thing, Cork's 3rd attempt—truck breaks down & they come back, I decide to go along & we split by 12 • Make it to Indio by 2 am, sleep 4 hours • Klondike, Squeak, Alan, Ruth tension, Peyton Place vibes • Just hanging out listening to music, smoke, take walks, get involved in closeness vibe, confusion bounce of the house walls, echoes, mind-wise soundings bounce trance to room walls, but feeling magnificent & sane • a lot of good meals, friendly, relaxed (still trying to hide parts of my reality, not acknowledge some realities—not in the Valley social scene, feel snobbish, go to Safford, get a drink, have a good time, find some weed, have a role in psycho-drama paranoia, strange but heavy impression—go for walks, shot a rabbit, went rock hounding, saw some old mines, went to pot-luck, good food but social claustrophobia, talk weed trip upstairs, back for xmas, get ready to go back—sad—caught • Thunderstorm in Globe, only ripple on trip, rest boring sameness • next day start same trip • Read & hang out—get school paper-work together—money worry, wonder if the trip is worth it at times—space, smoke lot of weed, makes one to catastrophize the energy, the lowest minds, contact, or interacting with outside social relations nil, makes for tension • Register for school, class ok, , later shuffling, try for financial aid, loans, school trips, paper—home again, still chaos • Week-end, kick back, go swimming, hock shop gun & binocs, food low, hassling Cork, mom not accept collect call • Buttons back, not mellow, no celebration, need job • Still smoking a lot of weed (Cork ¼ Lb)—welfare & slash pay the rent, only 135.00, screw Bob—borrowed 100.00, school fees

SEPTEMBER

Class drop & add, it's ok—borrow 60.00 for books, still no job, prospects gone but hanging out, Scott junk bunk & bullshit, cops, paranoia, PCP & insanity—no word from home, rumors, what are Squeak & Alan doing? Mom don't answer phone calls • Work in school progressing but no immediate money, so hustle—things working • Saw Debbie, a few sunsets, Katies Bday soon, money, groceries, cig., beer, Jeff, dope, read, rap, space, sleep • Katie's Bday, meal & cake, Cork drunk w/Sue • School, Buttons job card dealing, smoke, eat, rap, read, stereo • Skipped class, funky mood—Wells Fargo loan 915.00 8-10 wks, paperwork, space, thinking, changes, drunk, bike for sale • Woke tense, something missing, go to work 5 hrs, 10.00 meal—2 quacks high—Debbie & Charlie, more thinking, high, responsible • Corky to Yuba City • Ho hum, blues & doldrums in Chico City • M.C. card 300.00 credit, blow 100.00 • B.D. card Linda • Up to Cohasset, find notice for trailer • Bday Zachary A Luetkemeyer (Gene & Dianne) • Corky fight Jeff • Hassles w/Debbie • Ltr from Linda to Buttons, get trailer 175.00 to move in, Corky 170.00 unemp • Corky to Ariz

OCTOBER

Moving time again • moved to Cohasset • Paid 71.73 • Card to Sean for B.D., card to mom B.B., letter from mom, letter to Linda • Cards to Clancy, Buster & J.W., cut class • Quit work • BEOG 288.00 • Paid Nov rent 125.00 • Truck tune-up approx 25.00 • Got a dog, class • Class, changed oil, truck • Slow, hang out • Nothing • Skipped class, truck blew up • Skipped class • Test in anthro 101 • School, nothing special • Drunk at Greenwoods w/Tom Handy • Hangover, Halloween party

NOVEMBER

School, no V.A. check, wasted, Vinny from NY hitch ride • 42.00 OZ, skipped school • Geo quiz • MC 50.00, chk act 60.00 • drink beer, .22 out of hock, shoot cans • Build greenhouse, smoke, drink, eat, screw, read, breathe—Ah, life!! • Drink, eat, .22, walk, smoke, read, food—so this is it, huh? Life ain't easy, but it ain't hard • 120 chk act, sick • Doc, blood test, sick • Sick • Corky, bank loan (3 weeks), school, geo mid-term, better • Rain finally, cut wood, chain saw, rain, beer, food, real fine…

DECEMBER

So, folks, that's about all—drinking, school over, probably flunked a few but it was money…truck still fucked up, runs, but…• xmas great time, presents, food, champagne, cut a lot of wood w/Tom profitable relations—cut my hair, need a hat to keep my head warm • Loan of 908.66 + V.A. 396.00 = $1,304.66—spent all but 56.00, hope I had a good time; it sure was expensive • Card to the folks, a few back, weed from Alan, cans from Sandy, wok from Ariz people • X-mas vacation, lot of slow time, a few splurges & some rain • December 25, birthday—30 big ones—it's all downhill! • And so folks, 1976, not entirely bad but edited by bad habits, about bad habits—a lot of changes, a few fine moments & more good than bad—Till later, just passin' thru, Love is all, Chuck…

FROM 1977 JOURNAL

Wens Jan 11
grey foggy cool

Butcher rabbit, slow day, only 3 beers, Rich & Scottie by, Squeak zoom in
and gone again

thurs Jan 13

Foot mending; wish I could walk other than after a fashion—

Time, gray days, feeling old, attitudes piled in a corner like old clothes
unwanted, sitting in a going-to-goodwill box, now for the second month
these clothes are that unwanted—

Fri 13, moon pices
cloudy warm slow

ho hum day, bored, feeling sick & tired

Sat Jan 15

rain—more rain, quack!
sat & fri too, a total loss—must be what a state institution is like—just hang
out from time up to time down—quackers!

Clancy & Susannah came to dinner, had one of the roosters, tough as hell,
but tasty—Clancy to Peru in March...to Ariz? Sue to Sac to teach—changes

Dallas 27 to 10 Denver, Superbowl XII, whopper—rained all day, fuck

Mon Jan 17
still raining, raining

Ok day so far—butchered the white rabbit, should be tasty, plenty of meat,
marinate 48 hours—rain to flood the valley—saw some blue sky once! No
beer, 1st day

Tues Jan 18

2nd day no beer, ho hum day, school has to be an improvement as a time spender

Wens—a do nothing day, 3rd day no beer, do actually notice a change in body

Thurs—school registration—ok
1st beer in 3 days, saw Pattie & Trish

Fri sunny day, cloudy evening
dinner with Clancy, food & rest
horrible, the social trip, ho hum
Registered for school, 437 dollars, BEOG money

Sat, blah, watched the baby

Sun morn early
cold & sunny
up early, frost & ice but a sunrise—have to think about school trips, get in the proper frame of mind—money till 30 Mar, need some money trips—

Mon morn, 30 degrees
1st day of school, ceramics & Arabic, good class, take a while to remember all I used to know

Mon Jan 24

house broken into, weed & plant taken, fuck some types of people—Alan says Karma—he's right! Redneck Guru—

Tues, machine shop, drop later, Arabic easier, will be alright—like the teacher; changes

Wens, dropped metal, American Indian lit, need one unit, lunch w/Rich, walk the park

Thurs, clear, cold, restless, pawn 22 rifle, 15-17 Mar
need more energy, direction

Fri Jan 22 1977

Speedy day, music, clean-up, hour to Deb & C, plant garden, weed, need boxes, garage sale items, set up pig pen/feed, cut up oak, clean saw, kindling, restack wood, split logs—see squeak/store, empty trash burner, clean up garage, sort aluminum

Feb 8 1977

So January is gone—the blank pages were ones of hobbling around, broken metatarsal bone in left foot, my power foot, Capricorn goat hoof—drank too much, bullshitted too much, smoked too much, too much "too much"—today is the 8th of Feb, rest of unfilled pages can go into things to do, notes & observations, plans & memory jogs—lot of weirdness this new year, but around me, what center I have was not muchly affected—can't seem to get the proper trip w/school—keep see-sawing between redneck/hippie Cohasset vibes & the Chico responsibility/school trip—more energy to one or the other is needed—the ideas & knowledge side of school is far out, lot of energy, but the student trips, attendance, bureaucratic bullshit is fucking with my wa—more time to myself, more thought expression, write some more, smoke a little less—not bad, though, January…

Monday Feb 14, 1977

So Monday came & gone, still beautiful dry weather—went to school, nothing special, just need to get on the reading, one quiz down, two tests & two papers coming up—dreamt Alan sent some money & is coming out—also, Clancy showed up—will be interesting to see if anyone shows up—Buttons has a severe case of terminal living, poor girl is miserable—oh well, think today is bad, wait till tomorrow, it will probably be worse—

Thur Feb 17 1977

Winter is here, finally—more 70's this year than days of rain—even this storm is not a real storm, more a "Sears" storm, lot of work on the house—shower finally in, what a bitch old plumbing can be—Ruthie getting ready on her end—Buttons home sick, has been for the last few days—Squeak & Damien down wens—bought a new car on Chuck's credit, ought to be another story coming out of this—Corky coming back to Cal? Roxanne

moving to No. Calif? soap opera life—I must find a job or at least money—
life still sucks, huh!?—

Feb 18, 1977
Gemini moon
spacy? maybe

Got the ho hums—out of smoke, drinking my last beer & no job—but on the
up side I do have my shoes on, in case I need to actually go out and do
something—Buttons is still sick, also is profoundly affected by life & all its
trials, tribs & family—

FROM NOTEBOOK DATED "AS OF 26 APRIL 77"
PROBABLY ARIZONA

Wens am early sun in Taurus, moon in Leo/Virgo cusp
tea time sunrise time cool mornings lately fire going till 9 or so

Sat am early rain/sun/clouds cool moon virgo/libra cusp –
sore from walking but good nite's sleep feeling just fine

Thurs noon & sunny moon just past full just out of scorpio
kind of a quiet day but feeling a little mean

May 9 moon in Aquarius very wet rainy day just hanging
out in the trailer
watching the rain thinking things

May 26 moon in virgo Gemini B.D. Tom & Bar B Que & rain

June 26 Sun noon moon in scorpio –
very hot, dry day – no way to work outside probably go swimming again

11 July mon morning blues hangover again no sleep, one
of these days I'll learn – moon in Taurus the sun very hot, very bright,
no rain, all day

Sun July 24 moon Scorpio sun Leo, mellow
morning things to do been too lazy

Aug 7 Sunday afternoon moon Taurus/Gemini cusp, gathering of peoples
& energy time of departure traveling

Aug 17 wens moon virgo/libra rain today maybe kickback time planning
building energy harness time

Fri Aug 19 moon libra/scorpio ½ full clear no rain cool nites too dry

Wens morning Aug 31st Buttons B.D. moon
in Aries, Clancy shining, a job even, 2 even

16 sep moon Scorpio week-end Friday
nite really rainy cool/first fire in months
need to get a lot of things together

Nov 9 wens nite moon a last sliver
in Scorpio high energy day

Tues early morn moon cancer/sag sun 3 days
past full mostly clear cool moist winter is soon here

Dec 9 fri morn before sunrise clear & cold
moon scorpio/no quarter-skipping work/fucking off

Mar 6, 1978
clear/cloudy/cool

Thinking about moving to Ariz—summer jobs w/forestry 4.3.78—wrap up
trips here—

"Rotted slash"
May 17, 1978

So it's hip, hip, hippie hoo ray!
After all those years of dope smoking paranoia,
Long haired weirdness, changing scenes
& towns like a high priced whore changing
customers to suit her tricks, we find
that ultimate realization is sitting at
9000 feet in the White Mts of Ariz, grooving
on the surrounding forest & hoping that
the damned thing might burn down in order
to pick up a few days of overtime,
a bulging pocket full of silver from the
US Govt for a job and a forest well done.

CORKY REMEMBERS...

I

Klondyke, AZ, Summer, 1977

Chuckles and Bubbles went to Pinecrest, Az to work for the Forest Service. Chuck had fallen out of favor with the ruling class when he was unable to continue holding the four hundred pound engine block for the mechanic whose face was directly beneath it. I've forgotten how many facial fractures he sustained, but I guess some lingering malice about the incident remained. As luck would have it, Bubbles and Chuckles were in the only bar in Pinecrest that very afternoon, commiserating about the same when Johnny Paycheck's new song, "Take This Job And Shove It " came on the radio. It resonated with Chuck and was obviously a directive from his Spirit Guide.

24 hours later Chuck and Buttons descended on the peaceful little world of Klondyke. Buttons' 1952 Chevy truck needed a brake job and she was sporting a warning ticket from an AZ state trooper for going too slow on state highway 77. He had asked them if they were from the nearby San Carlos Apache Indian Reservation. Gee, they didn't look like Indians to me, although Chuck was wearing a bandana...

Chuck came in with six half racks of Hamm's. Beer supply was a critical issue as it was 50 plus miles on a dirt road to resupply. Chuck and I indulged in a contest to see who could drink the most beer before we ran out. Chuck won, but it wasn't completely fair because he started at 3:30 AM and I arose no earlier than five. By noon the following day we decided to go to Bonita to resupply. I took Buttons' brake shoes with me on the off chance we might find an old Chevy to salvage.

On the road to Bonita conversation shifted to potential employment as Chuck couldn't collect unemployment because he had quit his job (oh despicable system set up solely to annoy him!). Ideally he could find five weeks worth of employment, then get laid off and be able to collect unemployment on his Forest Service job for at least six months. Did I have any bright ideas?

At the time I was working as a cowboy (Cactus Cork) on leases retained by the Defenders of Wildlife (DOW) in the nearby Aravaipa Canyon, a scenic designated Primitive Area. My boss, Claude McNair, from a very old local ranching family, and whose politics were a little left of Nazism, was planning to send me into the wilderness to build trail between two line cabins. I would ask Claude if he would send Chuck with me to help me build trail. An unenviable job on the best of days. Chuck loved the idea!! I reminded him that it was grunt work (labor), and I would look bad in the community if he walked off the job in the middle of building trail. He assured me it was no problem and that he needed to get in shape anyway. I finished my beer at the Bonita bar/store whilst inquiring of the locals if anyone happened to have an old '52 we could cannibalize brake shoes from. Luckily, someone did. We went back to Klondyke and I called Claude that night with my proposal. He bought it! The next day Chuckles and I prepared to go to the line cabin. We repaired the brakes in Bubble's truck. Claude's son Butch, who was akin to Heinrich Himmler, showed up. After introductory pleasantries he took us to town for supplies.

The next morning, bumping along in the dark on an ancient trail converted to a "four wheel road", conversation was minimal. Butch had the personality of a house plant. Being the experienced cowboy that I was I made sure I sat in the middle. That made the far right passenger (Chuck) responsible for getting out and opening and closing the 37 gates along the four hour jeep trail to the line cabin. Said person was also responsible for bringing fresh cold beer from the ice chest to the other occupants. Welcome to cowboy etiquette. Chuck was still quite cheery as we approached the cabin. At this point I should mention a cultural peculiarity amongst AZ cowboys of the time. They considered it an absolute requirement to harass, cajole, intimidate, humiliate and laugh at every faux pas committed by any greenhorn (Chuck). It was a real three stooges approach to humor, and they were always looking for the fourth stooge. Getting a greenhorn to fall or get bucked off his horse was considered the highest form of entertainment. Needless to say Chuck did not consider himself a cowboy or a greenhorn.

We finally reached the line cabin for four weeks of trail building in the Aravaipa Wilderness Study Area. Ostensibly we had more than enough supplies for four weeks on Table Mountain. Butch marveled at what he considered to be the vast quantities of beer we had brought, to wit, 20 half racks. I thought it marginal, at best. Chuck was truly fearful. After Butch did his very best to put a dent in our beer supply, he left. "See you in three to four weeks" he yelled as he drove off. He had left us with another four wheel drive jeep which had been dropped off earlier in the week, two horses, Slipper and Socks, and adequate feed.

II

I took care of daily work tasks and animal care—horse catching, saddling and feeding. Chuckles didn't like horses, and he was afraid of them, although he would never admit it. He was in charge of all things food. When I got back to the cabin each morning after having fed and saddled the horses, Chuck would have breakfast ready. No matter what personal issues we might have had, He always took it upon himself to prepare a good meal.

The first couple of days went ok. We both worked hard and diligently. It was miserable, hard, stupid work though, what with moving rocks, cutting brush with dull axes, filling in potholes with rock and dirt (with shovels) and tamping it in with long steel tamping rods. Chuck kept imitating the apes in 2001, A Space Odyssey. *It got old for both of us right away.*

I tried to keep of us constantly aware of the ubiquitous rattle snakes. We were terrified of being bit out in the middle of nowhere and we always had an immediate evacuation plan in the event. After all, they'd left us with the horses and a jeep with a half tank of gas. That was just enough to get us both back to civilization So one day at the end of the first week, Chuck and I were rolling down the trail, horses in hand, tools in tow, when I heard Chuck say, "That one didn't rattle." It was a small black rattle snake, lethargic from the morning cold, straight across the path I had just stepped over. I jumped four feet. Chuck couldn't quit laughing, the prick. I killed the little bastard with rocks. When I went over to pick it up, Chuck shouted, "You better check it with a stick first, ya dumb ass"! I did and the little shit struck the stick!!! To this day I credit Chuck with saving my life. We would never have got back to civilization in time. Thank God for Chuck. I did, however, retain a small resentment against him for laughing at me, even though he saved my life; isn't that the way people are sometimes?

One day the following week, after grueling trail work in the sun since 5 AM, we knocked off around 3:30 PM. We took showers in Chuck's home made coffee can shower contraption, then contemplated our latest dilemma. Namely, we were running out of beer! Chuck suggested we go back to Klondyke in the jeep, go to Bonita, get more beer and return. I had to remind him of current cowboy etiquette. I would be subject to ridicule and humiliation for returning early for beer. Chuck responded, "So what are you worried about? That they'll think we drink too much beer? Yes, I replied, and came up with an alternative suggestion. Why don't we go over to San Manuel, on the other side of the mountain? I said. It was on a different jeep trail, they didn't know us over there, and no one on our side need ever know. He loved it! It had the right amount of intrigue and deception to thrill the both of us.

I drove. Chuck was in charge of opening gates. Two hours later we arrived at the saddle, a pass in the San Manuel Mountains and the passage down to San Manuel and beer. We were met by a monsoon, a full-blown horrific thunderstorm. Rain and hail poured in every direction. We proceeded, intent on our mission. The fierceness of the storm increased. As we came to the rise, Chuck said, "Ya see that tornado off in the distance?" I replied,

"We don't have tornados in Arizona." Lightening bolts were striking every three to four feet on either side of us, like what I imagined an artillery barrage to be. As we approached the first gate on the road to San Manuel, Chuck deferred on the side of caution; he refused to get out and open it. I appealed to his manhood; I called him a coward and other despicable filthy names, but to no avail. He said I ought to get out and open the gate. He didn't need a beer that bad. Cursing him and all his progeny, we returned to the cabin WITHOUT BEER! Resentments began to multiply.

We entered our final week of trail building anxiously awaiting our return to civilization...and BEER. I remember Chuck going out of the cabin two mornings before our rescue, pointing to the mountain view outside our cabin, and saying, "Isn't that majestic?" I said "Yeah, right!" The day before our pickup, remembering Chuck laughing over my near miss with the black rattlesnake, I decided to play a trick on him. Remember, Chuck really didn't like horses; in fact he was scared of them. So after a grueling, hard day of labor in the hot sun, we headed back to the cabin. As we approached, I kicked the horses into a gallop and headed for the low trees, hoping Chuck would get sheared off and land on his ass! He didn't, but turn-around is fair play! Thus ended our stay on the mountain.

Corky Owens, Brother-in-law
Elk Grove, CA, June 1, 2008

Tris, Sean, Chuck, Pacific Grove 1978

One of my fun memories is of when Chuck & Buttons took Sean with them during the summer. Sean was probably around 5 yrs old. I believe they were based in Chico at the time. At some point they dropped me a note and asked when they should bring Sean home. My reply was in the form of a postcard. I simply said, "Keep him till he's 18." Needless to say, I wasn't serious but to the very end, he remained Uncle Chuck. He remains a very colorful character in our family.

Michele

OPPOSING MOJOS

It was 1981. Chuck and Buttons lived in Berkeley and they and Leslie and I often threw the I-Ching coins. Vibes were weird then; it was a time of chaos and dark looming shadows. Chuck and Buttons were in frequent opposition, their bickering poisoning the air. One day Chuck gave me his I-Ching coins, which were kept in a nylon draw-string bag. The coins contained his mojo, he said, and it was a good mojo, since the coins were being given in a sentimental moment. Later I told Buttons about the gift. She said, "Yeah? Well, I put a curse on them! If you ever use them, bad shit will happen!" They now contained her mojo, too, evil mojo. I never used them after that. I still have them, 27 years later. They sit on a shelf in my office. Sometimes at night I can hear the coins clattering inside the draw-string bag as the opposing mojos battle for control.

GETTING THE POINT IN BERKELEY

It was about that same time. We were in the Berkeley apartment where we cut and weighed and packaged the product. We'd been up for two days snorting and debating the metaphysics of hard times, becoming crazier by the hour. Chuck was getting testy, wanting to prove a point. I was long past knowing what the point was, something about being real, about how you are going to act when you're up against it, when the shit is real, when it hits the fan. I may have said I wasn't sure of the point. He said something like, You want the point? You want the fucking point? And he pulled out his Buck knife, which he was fond of carrying in those days, and flipped open the blade and pushed my head back and put the point of the blade against my neck and said something like, Here's the point, dipshit! What are you going to do now? I did nothing, there was nothing to do, it wasn't my move. I may have said something to that effect, that I would do nothing, it wasn't my move. He kept the blade there and rambled a while, I don't remember about what, then removed the blade, as I knew he would when he felt that he'd made his point. I hadn't been worried; it was just Chuck being Chuck.

Gene

ANY WHERE, ANY TIME!

It was 1981, the Bay Area. Things were not going well in my life and my business. My behavior was erratic, the end was near. Chuck lived in Berkeley and was working for me then and saw it unraveling, saw chaos dancing in the shadows. He may have felt guilty, partly responsible, because he was supposed to be helping me out and his help wasn't helping. In the peculiar way that guilt transforms to a defensive, outwardly directed anger, Chuck became aggressive toward me. One day he left a message on my answering machine. It went something like: "You want a piece of me? You think you can take me? I'll meet you anywhere, anytime, Bro! In a fucking alley, on a street corner, under a street light! Anywhere, anytime!" It was a drug-induced schizoid drunken ramble. There was no particular precipitating incident, so it was bizarre and sad but funny, too. I saved it for a while, and would listen sometimes and could only wonder. I thought of saving it for posterity, or at least until times were better, the chaos behind us, and we could listen together and laugh, but I accidentally erased it. Had I not, I could have played it for him on one of his final days in the hospital. "Anywhere, anytime!" he would have heard himself say. "How about now?" I might have said. He would have appreciated the humor. And then again, maybe not...

Gene

Inside the Antique Shop, *Old Habits*, Arcata, CA, 1980 Something

I ALWAYS GET MY MAN

It was 1983. Chuck lived in Chapman Town, Chico, CA. He was standing on his porch drinking a beer when a black sedan pulled up and a man in a black suit and dark glasses got out and said, "Are you Charles Bernard Luetkemeyer?"

"Who wants to know?"

"Agent xxx of the Northern California Office of the FBI," the man said, whipping out his badge. "I'm assigned to your brother's case. Have you seen him lately, Charles?"

"Fuck off!"

"Charles, you tell your brother we consider him armed and dangerous. If he resists arrest, we will shoot to kill." The agent pulled open his suit coat, revealing his holstered weapon.

"You hurt my little brother, mother fucker, and you will deal with me!"

"Don't be stupid, Charles. You tell your brother that I'm assigned to his case and I always get my man. Do you understand? Here's my card, Charles, in case you forget my name." He held out his card. Chuck let it fall to the ground. The agent walked back to his car. He turned and said, "Tell him I always get my man!"

When Chuck related the incident to me that same day on a pre-arranged payphone to payphone call, he seemed especially proud of how he had told the agent to fuck off, that if he hurt his little brother, he'd deal with him! I was proud of that, too. Though the danger was real and not mitigated by bravado, it made me feel good that I had a big brother who was looking out for me and would stand up to any threat to keep me safe.

The agent, by the way, did not get his man.

Gene

The Ayatollah Stare, Time & Place Unknown

With Chuck several words come to mind: volatile, intense, challenging and Chico. Chuck was a very challenging person. He especially liked to challenge his siblings and it was a challenge just to be around him sometimes. He was very honest, always told the truth, brutally sometimes, but the truth nonetheless. He didn't like bullshit, but he did like to dish it out. I always felt a little intimidated by his intensity, like he was going to explode at any moment. If anyone has ever been to Chico, California, and knows what it's like to live there, that's Chuck. They really should name a street after him. He was born to be a Chicoian. I couldn't imagine him living anywhere else.

Dianne Hudson, Ex-sister-in-law
Austin, TX, May 7, 2008

134

Dad, Illinois, 1966: The Source Of The Ayatollah Stare

135

Tris, Ortanna, June 1983

I remember "really" meeting my Dad when I was seven. (I know I saw him before but I don't remember those times) Mom and I took a train trip out to California. I was thrilled to be meeting my Dad! It was kind of like a feeling of belonging, if that makes any sense.

My dad treated me ok. There were long times when I didn't hear from him, but at the same time, the phone/letters went both ways. I didn't go out of my way to contact him either. It was like he had his life with his family and I had mine. I know he loved me, though! In the early days of our relationship he was just "my Dad", although I do recall calling him "Chuck" for a period of time, because I wasn't sure if I should call him "Dad" or not.

Since I wasn't around him a lot, I can't really say how he changed over the years. He didn't seem as angry in his later years as he did when I was around him when I was a teenager. I guess he mellowed out! I think we came to an understanding that neither of us was angry or hurt by lost time.

136

Circumstances were what they were, and life went on. I think he knew that he was important to me and I know that I meant a lot to him.

One of my favorite times with my Dad was in June, 2004. My best friend Becky and I drove out west for the summer and it was the first time I had been with my Dad on Father's Day.

There was a time when he made me mad. This happened when Dad and Buttons were living in Anacortes, Washington. I went out for a visit and had only been there a short time, perhaps a couple of weeks. Dad had a dog, Tragar. Tragar puked on my brand new luggage! Being an emotional teenager, this really upset me. My Dad thought it was funny. This set me off even more (I definitely inherited his temper, and I ended up leaving and going to Michele's in California for the rest of my visit out west.)

I was bothered most by my Dad's drinking. I have a hard time being around people who can't handle their alcohol. But truthfully, he never got angry with me. And his sarcasm and cynicism never bothered me. Not really...I'm pretty much the same way. Except for the outright cynicism part. I keep that mostly to myself, I guess. But I can be very sarcastic at times. Talia has even picked up on it and says things that crack me up at times. My dad would have loved being around her.

I think he was a gifted writer and I always looked forward to getting a letter or card from him. I liked the way he wrote about the world. And he gave me some good advice: Don't eat yellow snow!

I would like to have known more about him. I would like to have had him know more about me and Talia.

Tristessa, Daughter
Tennessee, June 16, 2008

STATIONS

Paper is so cheap, so plentiful
   that I knowingly can afford
     to waste
the backside of pages—

like the Catholic church warning
   of the thousands of souls
flushed, douched
   or otherwise wasted

during unsanctioned sex
   & masturbation,
that I, cocksure
   & city street Buddha

I take the words
   of "save-the-tree-ers",
& dance with them, confetti-like
   upon the passing parade of life—

Life will grow regardless
   tho all of man
     may soon crumble
under the moss squeezing
   down upon the concrete—

Hydrochloric acid is used to
   etch lines upon glass,
patterns of man's handling
   scratched deep upon the surface—

I wonder what alcohol
     has etched upon my liver,
the dates of my passing,
     or a suicide note

pinned upon my chest
     like a Chinese laundry slip,
or a note passing a young child
     from one station to another—

A TINY VOICE

Somewhere deep
     inside of Alan Watts
must have been a tiny,
          tiny voice
 screaming to be heard,
     heard just once
before I drowned in alcohol—

THINGS HAPPEN!

Life goes on all around me,

just as I sit
    & pass from one day
to another,

so does life also
    just sit & pass
        the time,

while all around it
    green pushes through the earth
& things happen—

I sit in the dark,
    patiently planting seeds
        of tomorrow's hangover,
while the plants sleep
        & await tomorrow's sun—

HEY, CHUCK, FUCK OFF!

I can think of no one
who cares enough for me,
or me for them,
to write a letter—

So then,
 maybe I should write
 a suicide note,
 a laundry list,
 notes of things to do,
or just wait for the holidays
and send out cards?

If I wasn't so bored
 so hung up on myself,
I'd try to write some poetry,
 or work up the feeling
to tell everyone to just
 Fuck Off!!

Hey, Chuck—
 Fuck Off!
Leave these people (& myself) alone—

Chuck With Unknown Companion, probably Chico, mid-eighties

NOTES ON A FARSIDE CALENDAR, 1985

JANUARY

So, it's another year—happy! I'm working, the weather sucks, Ruthie's in the hospital—a heart attack • On x-mas day Corky skipped out on me, owes me 400.00—I'm really pissed • He fell off the wagon, doing heroine & stealing everyone blind—I don't know what to do; kicking his ass won't solve anything—Squeaky is doing massive weirdness; her boy friend got a dildo stuck up his ass, w/the batteries on & humming • I wish I had never met an Owen—I'm sick of assholes & weird people—oh, well! • Meanwhile it is go to work, be a jerk—brown shoes don't make it • The weather alone is enough to depress a saint—rain, rain, rain • We don't need to run to the ocean & drown—god brought the ocean to Chico, we can drown here • Still working, tax day comes & goes—my tax money fell into a hole in Corky's arm

FEBRUARY

Clancy, Connor, Buttons, Lucille & Buel are off to Scotty's—Sunny day, almond trees starting to blossom—Bud, my vegetarian pit bull, loves the rivers so much, he won't get in the car; I chase him ½ mile & back • Get up, go to work—Corky comes over while I'm gone & O.D.'s—cops & EMT, Buttons in a rage, kids in hysterics—K.T. takes the kids and they are going back to Florida—another day as the world turns • Cold, grey, windy, winter is back—a ho hum day, go to work, come home, have a beer, hear Damien is looking for a place to live, Squeak the Geek won't take him & he won't stay where he is; see what I mean? Ho hum—

Leslie & Buttons, 1985

What I will remember of Chuck are memories of a huge, burly man holding a beer, standing with a group of friends, a button-down Hawaiian shirt of rayon loosely covering his barrel chest as his long, wiry hair blew in the wind. Thick, massive eyebrows furrowed either in judgmental thought or in skeptical observation. He was a man of opinion and quick to voice it.

I remember him in the corner chair, holding his morning tea, finishing a novel begun early that morning while most of us slept.

Although these memories are just a few that I hold for Chuck, they are the ones I choose to remember.

Leslie Luetkemeyer, Sister-In-Law
Clayton, CA, May 9, 2008

144

By Buttons Old Pick-up, Time & Place Unknown

Chuck, Buttons, Linda, Michele, Chico, CA 1980 something

My first impression was that Chuck was intriguing and very pleasant to look at. After all, he was a Capricorn. My personal history is an attraction to Capricorn men but it's very difficult to handle the Goat energy.

Chuck did his best to be very pleasant throughout our entire interactions with one another. It was my feistiness that would cause some distance...as I did not always agree on how he dealt with his ladies. Not that it was necessarily my business but our lives were intertwined. He was always a brother..."

Michele

Linda, Tris, Chuck, Time & Place Unknown

Inside The Pagoda Of Point Defiance, Anacortes WA, 1989

I spent a good deal of time with/around Chuck when he lived with Buttons in Anacortes Washington in the late 80's and I lived in Lakewood. Chuck, Buttons and Tragar, their pit bull, all lived in a small green and white house off the road headed for the ferry. They both seemed happy then until they both got jobs working on a juvenile detention island.

About that same time, for Bridgie's and my wedding reception, we hired Chuck and Buttons to cater, $200 apiece and all the party favors that they wanted and a motel for the night. It was a fun day. They had come down to Tacoma before and stayed. Bridgie, being a recovering alcoholic, was not pleased with their lifestyle but an Indian RN that she worked with that came to dinner a couple of times, shot his wife and kids one Sunday, so she was no great judge of people.

Leroi Moody, Friend
Edwardsville, Il, June 8, 2008

148

April 6.90 Virgo Moon
Happy Birthday Dad

Jimmy Buffett evening—calypso beat, Cajun chatter—slightly transplanted to the Pacific Northwest—I mean, we were headed for Jamaica, took a 180 wrong turn somewhere in Illinois or Missouri and ended up in Wash state—

Sometimes, all that happens seems to be just a flowing outward ripple; slowly, exactly moving out from some point that becomes centered simply due to the fact of its happening; its central existence defined by the pattern that comes after—even before the center exists at all, the outward flowing pattern defines that existence—because of that flowing pattern of ripple, the center comes into being—
if it weren't for the yama-yama…

> …bullshit
> would just be
> another splash
>   frozen
> in the reality
>   of life—

SPLASH

> I want to be
>   a rock & roll
>   singer
> I want to tell
>   people
> how to see
>   life
> as a poem

> I want them
>   all to be poets—

> All of life
>   is to be sung
> melody of emotion

When the words
        become awkward
                or even fail
                        altogether,
let the emotions
        arrange themselves
        into chaos
or just vibrations
        faintest
even the faintest
        of ripples
excite the air

passing outward
        from the center
as water rolls
        slowly from
the center
        of a splash

Voice becomes
        song
as the sounds
        push outwards
from the center
        of a feeling
        an idea
        an emotion

be so goddam
        glad
you can read
        this,
feel anything
        at all—
and become
        the ripples
spreading outward
        from that splash

of yourself w/life

Can you
        read this?
Did you
        just read
                that?
You have just
        become centered
realized
        all there
                is
to
        reality

Did you just
        go
                what?
        or
did you lose
        it—huh?

Welcome
        to
                the
                        fucking
        "Ocean
                of
                        life
                                café!"
Quit your bitchin'

Of course
        you
                are
                        going
                to die!
You just read
        that,

right?

So!
Give thanks
        to God!

That's all you get,
time after time after time

If you're not
        dead,
and
        you're not,
Breakfast
        today
                will be:

cold cereal & banana

if that pisses you
        off
praise God, you're
        alive

Quit your
        bitchin
& have another
        banana—

        Thanks for
        stopping by
        for breakfast!

                Chuck
                4.6.90

NITE AT JED'S
4.24 Aquarius moon
clear almost sunny –

Hey, just a fuckin' drunk
    another nite at Jed's
very important to get this down right

Starting to get crowded – louder –
    people coming in,
    lots of recognition
"hellos & how are yous"

The jukebox gets louder
    the music speeds up
        a decade or two
slightly familiar in style
    totally unknown
        as to authorship

it's not so much
    who are these people?
as it is
    why are they
        saying that
            like that ?

It can't be noise
    If you could ask them
they
    wouldn't know
        what

    are you talking about?!

Is it so much
    misunderstanding
or youth?
    Maybe youth—Somewhere

                    underneath the noise
                        there is someone
                    saying something!?

Underneath
            there is
                    a mellowness
all the contrary
                For the noise –

This screaming
                    silent understanding

So it is a little after ten –
And—sex, drugs & rock & roll,

                    Are what!
                        Are what?

A coherence,
            a bonding

such a separate-ness
                & conversation's
loud
            louder than
                        music
except

the control of
the volume
blending

so you play the juke box
                    yourself
maybe change the flow
            you grab their attention
                    the music does mean something

a picture of the bar

must begin w/the lady
    tending bar

the music
    does not give her power –

no one
    is caught in the change
        the flow
to most
    it must be
        just noise

but,
    "This is the end"

another voice
    from so long ago

always here –
    from the jukebox
    from the music
always here – "this is the end"—

So do we write this
    as a poem
or is it a letter
    to you?

Jed's – 1992
    The Doors 1970
Jim Morrison
    As real as…
        The end!!!

"and he
    walked on down the hall!"

So twenty years ago

these kids
        shared these sentences
           w/Dr. Spock

and now
      is this just screams
          from the past
    or – the scream
         from a butterfly –

there was
      a whole generation
a whole belief
      in this –

"this is the end,
      beautiful friend"

So, just a song…

20 July Sag
Secret Harbor, WA
warm sunny cloudy

Mind's so warped
as to become Euclidean

Well, it's Jed's again, last bar before the water—a tavern across from the Dakota shipyards, where there certainly ain't no turistas—pool, darts, burgers & beer, all the black sheep of the babyboom—one of the better jukeboxes for the old hippies on the west coast.

I'm waiting for the boat; almost more of a concept than a statement—depending on how the children are behaving, how the tides are running & the winds are blowing, it may or may not be on time or even there at all. Like I say, "If you're on the boat, you caught it at all!" Trying to get a boat to Secret Harbor is like tossing "cast your fate to the wind" & "pissing in"…the same…excuse me, but I'm literally rambling; comes from splitting a pitcher w/myself on a hot day in a dark bar—it's probably 76 degrees out, supposed to climb to 80-85—around here that kind of heat can kill more people than hypothermia—everyone from around here has an Uncle Bernie who died fishing off Alaska, frozen solid in his survival suit, or an Auntie Pam, who collapsed of prostration while gossiping & whining with the check-out lady in Safeway—

So, I figure on getting to the dock early enough so it it's late enough & I'm drunk enough, I can be mellow enough to face the old lady & her old lady and the kids—besides, if I miss the boat, then I'm still here—I've got a few bucks and I can sleep in the van and if I have to be here, well something might happen, it always does—

22 July, Cap

STUMPY & THE BOAT THIEVES

A stranger comes in
  a conversation
a suicide in the park
  a conversation w/Pattie/Eric
a proposition & a plea
a cook, a druggie & P.I.
  sucker for a cause
  angry for the young man

Walking to the dock
  stolen bikes& lady cops
another conversation
  around to suicide
and pills & the drug scene
  mountain bikes & mother-in-laws

Back to the island
  the tide's in—
        Walton the wonder boy
        and his guns
  children & the outlaw Illuminati
        Stumpy & the Boat Thieves
  dishwashers & prep cooks
        & pirates

The kids alumni
        Stump & Rob, guns & neuroses
  the real gangsters
        cargo containers of coke
        bales of pot

WIND PARTING FOG

Man, can you sometimes get into
country type music—the melodies
all seem to play a relaxed, slowed-down,
almost a sad type of feeling—
memories glimpsed through a fog
like a building seen through
the mists floating on the river,
the winds, for a second, part the fog
and we catch impressions of the warehouses,
long ago built upon the piers
and now old and decayed, crumbling
and falling into the brown river—

STROBE POEMS

My dad's dead,
why not my habit?

      □□□

Consider airplanes & helicopters,
      those things are up there
for a reason –

Flying dead center
      down the Guemes Channel
electronic array
      signaling the sound –

Sonar sounding,
      submarine warfare—?

It's done for a reason!

      □□□

Another walk on the beach –
      Oh, fuck!
            I look up—a Doberman!
                  If you're afraid of dogs…

She is as dainty
      as a deer
as aware, prancing
      silently, aggressively!

Her owner
      waits behind,
          also aware,
             wary

Leather & chain

           dangle from his hand

And then
     they too
          are gone –

               □□□

So you're just sitting there
          and they walk by
him all macho-stepped
          her awkward & tentative stepped
working to work within his swagger

               □□□

3.22
2nd day of spring
glorious, tulip bloom, spring

so the world is just beautiful
               the 2nd day of spring
          people respond
                    buds unfolding
          as sweet a mystery
                    as themselves,
          little old ladies –

today
     all the men lag behind
          an idiot voice or two,
     but
          ignored
               unheard

                    Chuck 3.21.92

FROM A NOTEBOOK MARKED "PERSONAL 92"

5.8 Friday sunny/hazy
I-5 Oregon, going south

So it's that time of the year again – spring has sprung and possibilities are growing towards summertime –

We are in a rest spot on I-5 – Buttons is watching tv, catching up on her soaps – I'm watching the big 360 & writing this down – this rest area is jammed, quite busy, the last two shut down because of road construction – being an election year there are lots of federal/state funds being recycled back down to the people – for all the good of it, it is still irritating, the political ads & clown shows on & in the media these days – every 50 – 75 miles, someone decided that this and that spot would be a perfect place to slow traffic to a crawl, the better for a person to see how his & her monies are being spent – in the interest of social graces, are we supposed to say thanks?

The amount of traffic on this freeway is impressive – after two years on an island w/only 3 trucks & a tractor the only vehicles, not all running at the same time, ever, this is a major culture/reality shock – 3 & 4 lanes north & south, very constant traffic – lots of commercial vehicles, semi-rigs, logging trucks, plus the tourists, w/all the vans & Winnebagos, trucks, cars, all pulling cars & vans & trailers & such –

I'm noticing these especially since what we are 'on the road' in is basically that – a large truck towing a large travel trailer – we rented the u-haul w/the money we got from selling our old dodge van; hooked up the trailer, bought w/an IRS refund check; and so they say "parted these parts in search of a more favorable climate…"

So, we are once again self-contained, self-oriented and very self-motivated – a truly lazy person will never rest, until he can, until he can-

So, we are two weeks off of the Island; two days & 300 miles into this travel; and sitting in a rest stop in Oregon – the trees are hard woods & green, the birds are not sea birds, the mountains are different; so far from the ocean, the air is sweeter, more a spring fragrance than the salt tang of cypress Island—

162

5.9 sunny cool
outside Yreka, Mt Shasta

High plains, all sage & jack-rabbits and old Indian vibes – volcanic formations not extinct at all, some major eruptions in the area as recently as 1915 – not to worry – east of here, on towards Nevada, the land is really primitive, Modoc County where they had Captain Jack, another renegade Indian, held up for a year or two – actually he held them up, frustrated a couple of army expeditions for almost two years – came down on his own, and they hung him anyhow – no sense of honor –

The Indians that lived around here were great warriors amongst real bush league Indians – they would advance in a line against a similar line of whatever enemy was the enemy at that time and commence to sing songs & insults to one and other, occasionally shooting arrows at each other – when a couple were riled to passions of frenzy, they would dance out to each other and bash each other with clubs (the same clubs they used to hunt rabbits with) – In the background were all the women whose job it was to collect the men wounded on the plains, also all the arrows laying around – after a while both sides had enough blood & gore to color up their stories in the evening when all were sitting around the cooking fires; and they would quit and do just that, sit around the fire & bullshit about the....oh well, lost the story here-

6.8 Virgo moon
  Cool hot sunny

So, now we are at the Chapman Center, 4 years later than the last time—a bear, a book, $5.00 in my pocket, someone playing "Mighty Diamonds" reggae; this being the 3rd world hub, this Chapmantown—shades of California to come, when the white man becomes a minority for the first time since we conquered the Mexican/Spanish and finished off whatever Indians were still left –

Back in Chico—another bike, another summer—nothing to do, lots of time to do it in—

163

24 June raining, cool
Cohasset in the pines—

        The monkey is watching you;
            The animal is out there—

Sept 7 Katies's birthday
Coolish, maybe 85 degrees, sunny

        So, Leroy—

            K—pa—so—again—amigo—
        Here—is & have—a happy
            Wedding day for you
            & of course your daughter
            and even her old man!

    And so
            The moon slides from Capricorn to Aquarius—
    A Virgo sun
            Keeps a sort of order—
    We are talking fun that started
                            Out
            Willful, moving on
                    To a cheerful acceptance

        Actually it was just a birthday but
        With a Virgo correctness—

    K.T. has, on her 25th B.D., a boyfriend from So. Africa—
he's white; but the whites got there in the 1500's & some good time Charlie
Zulu got there not long afterward, & he has the flare at the nostril & an odd
slant at the eye—her last boyfriend was a neo-nazi and some real person
from So. Africa is more than welcome—he is also a chiropractor; cracks
jokes, necks, tension—

        You have a daughter either done it or doing it, marriage I mean—does
it make you wonder about things; not just wedding, presents,

                                                        164

reception, ...but—wow—no girl gets married without being born of a father—you can't get past the fact that time has really been a factor here—if your baby grows up and does this, well pretty much everything grew up and got older too!!

Woke up this am, sept 7, 6 am & watched the Boys from Illinois, 'The Blues Brothers' – "How much for your wife" – you know of course that the wife was already out of her chair & going along – but the boys from Illinois only wanted the horn player – she is still waiting and wanting to go – during this scene Pee Wee Herman was the waiter who brought the champagne to the table—

So Katie is 25 – the dog is deaf – we have a new cat, a real macho kit – he bites! He is a master of the Ho Chi Min ambush – hack & slash/run and fight again/make you bleed a thousand & a thousand cuts –

So we have 2 palm trees, a small stand of black bamboo –
I'm a registered democrat

I have a wife, an ex-wife, a step daughter, a daughter, 3 ex old lady/shack ups a year or 2, my sister is a grandmother, my bro's and sisters have children, my friends are getting old, their kids are having kids –

My last name means "a small landowner" – I have a 15 yr mortgage on a 7,100 sq ft lot – a sure small walk around a definition –

So, in 46 days I will be 46 yrs old; born in 1946, been here everyday since –

Gordon Lightfoot—musical vibes; another man getting older – a bit schmaltzy but he plays the notes the way an old man would chip facets off of another diamond – as repetitious as an everyday thing, the ever growing pile of diamond dust & debris making a hazy, joking sort of distraction –

Getting to be an old geezer, according to the kids – my biggest adventures these days are short walks through my check book; trying to reconcile my economy with the realities of everyday life – I seem to always have what I need, can find where the rest is coming from and manage to hold...

Katie, Time & Place Unknown

If there was one thing Chuck was, he held a fucking grudge and when he was wronged, he would have told the pope himself to fuck off. Believe it or not, I'm more like chuck than anyone else you'll ever meet.

Katie, Daughter
Roseville, CA
October 15, 2006

Zoe, Daughter Of Katie, Time & Place Unknown

If there was ONE person on the planet Chuck loved more than anyone, it was Zoe, even more than me. The sun rose and set on her.

Katie, Daughter

CANDLE

Candle, candle
    burning bright
know you then,
    these wanderers of night
all the cursed who sit alone
    so dead & cold
and staring,

staring out
    into the night,
receiving not
    the faintest of warmth,
nor feeling the rosy flush of wine,
    nor the heat of summers night
from this reflection
    of the candle burning bright
there upon the black pane
    of window glass
put between the world & me,
    all of things must pass—

PART III

1993 – 2006

SUBSTANCE

A blank piece of paper,
    liken it unto
a blank canvass;
    an afternoon,
blue sky & grassy hills,
    both sliding to meet the sea—

this time given over
    to a quiet mind,
an afternoon of daydreams—

a sketchpad,
    quick lines drawn blackly,
just a border

    for ideas
            that dance just ahead,
straining for substance—

1.22.93 Sunny finally
Aquarius/Aquarius

The sun is finally out, weeks of heavy & constant rain—the drought is over—welcome back to Calif—brought a bit of Washington State back with us, it seems—

So today: We are planning a garden—checking the boundaries, getting an idea, a conceptual image of how to do it—rained out!

Thinking about going back to work, what a drag that is—knowing the J.O.B is out there; waiting, worse than a golem, Frankenstein is a weenie—the J.O.B. is "bad"—and I am working hard at making myself as attractive as a goat in a clearing, a victim waiting on the pyre—

Listening to the next door neighbor's music program this afternoon, 3:50 pm; almost rap, 14-16 yr old music, heavy on the bass—When dad is home, it is mariachi & salsa—he plays the trumpet, dad does...

So—Buttons is in Monterey—her & Corky & Ruthie—everyone all made-up from the holidaze & the annual fighting—

Clancy comes by here; we toast the marriage & the baby with some homebrew—life goes on, as only can be known by having gone on—beer & babies, part of the on-going life cycles; with the beer though, I won't have to wait as long before it matures—

So—how about a state of the union address here: House, still owe 52,000.00...the foundation structurally is fucked—the yard is 1/6 of an acre and so far is not under water—The cops want part of my time, a chunk of the money I don't have, and I don't agree with them at all...Buttons & I have no jobs, not a hell of a lot of enthusiasm, but more than enough Mojo to pull this off—If we can do all this without actually doing anything, then Mojo must count for something—

1.24.93 cold clear skies
"How you jivin' w/that cosmic debris?"

Kicking out the jams w/some vintage Frank Zappa...way back when, 60's-70's, we rocked & rolled to this music; who would have thought that it would piss off our kids as well as our parents! Last time I heard any live Zapp was an interview in 1991; seems during a broadcast radio interview in Seattle at a young-progressive-rock college station, seems they asked him not to smoke pot in the studio, not because they were anti-marijuana, au contraire, these babies are from the hip parents of 60's-70's—no, they objected to the effects of second-hand smoke, said ol' Frankie could fire up down the hall outside, away from folks what breathe—did we miss the point here, us old geezers—how can we be so cool & yet, so incorrect—

1.28.93
foggy cool grey→dismal

Another sunrise, sort of, actually more of a greyer, lighter sort of, as dark as it was! So, today being the 5th day of me being the major 'asshole' of a few people's conceptual continuity—the very same as before; I mean my karma is caught in a revolving door; the further I go the faster I stay there—spinning my wheels; fish or cut bait or fish or...mixing metaphors could describe my mental state—

Major problems, major decisions about practically everything in my life—the only thing I am sure about is that all of this happened before & before and I'm still dealing w/it and I'm totally bummed because I can't figure out how to break this cycle—no matter what I do or how I do it, nobody is satisfied, including myself; I wouldn't mind someone actually telling me just what the point is; what the rules are; are we even playing by the rules, those rules being made up by the other player, whose conceptual continuity is that they don't have any rules at all—So, this makes sense? Play w/your own rules and explain to yourself and to the other folks in the game just what those rules are—if after all this, you end up being left alone on your field, either go find another game, or stay there and find some other players—

When I left Chico, I was glad to be gone—I'm back after 4 years and it's starting to seem like the same—only some problems getting worse, some resolved, but soon replaced with more of the same—

Jan 31, 1993 Superbowl Sun
Sunny, high energy, Taurus moon

They won't allow gays into the military, but they let Michael Jackson into the Super Bowl?? I miss the point here, what's the difference? Easy—M.J. doesn't get to touch the ball; come on, Colin Powell, take a chance—

2.21.93 from one storm→another
cold & grey, Pices/Pices

> "When I took up his offer, I must have been mad"
> Ol' Bobby Zimmerman

Everyone has to go chasing down the Nile, looking for Jewels—for the people who don't know what they are looking for, eternally blessed, they find nothing—if you knew & didn't find anything, would the journey itself be enough—to travel your whole life, would this once-in-a-lifetime journey be enough of its own reward? Would this answer then be the only jewel, just another jewel?

JUNE 2.93
Scorpio moon, rain

Just another job interview—waiting for the boss—very busy place—class & quality & casual—great big loaves of homemade bread, coffee drinks & muffin eaters—ought to be interesting—weird hours for me, but what the heck, huh?—need lights for the bike, reflectors—

Busy place—must generate a lot of bread, so to speak—checks on time?? A step up for the working man—

Birkenstocks & casual—older crowd or maybe the students are just gone, people wanna-be's w/no humility—children on bicycles, playing at being adults, probably grow up to be just like someone else—

A lot of changes in just a couple of days—walk off one job—get an interview the next day; go to work the same day? A person moves into the backyard—money, trouble, "room mate" hassles? Changes for sure—a job downtown, but evenings, after hours w/o the crowds—a large crowd of employees, after the V. Café, w/absolute min to 10—? people all moving w/purpose & dispatch—

172

Waiting, waiting, waiting…

Impressions so far—busy, confidence, of course it is still just a job—someone washes the dishes, mops the floors & carries out the trash—the crowd, the customers, Calif. casual—art gallery & the chronicle to go with their coffee—

A kid w/grandpa—kids are always kids & grandpas do grandpa things with them—when do kids stop being their age

April 6 93 warm hazy
Happy birthday Dad!

So another day! Finally went back to work—no money, no benefits, another greasy spoon; a dysfunctional possibility

2.28.93 pices/Gemini
sunny/warm; Chuck sucks

So I quit a job before I even had it – I work one day, decide I don't like it, decide not to take it, and everyone is "disappointed, pissed, bummed, disgusted & suffering a small amount of loss"…

Myself: a bit of guilt, more than a modicum of ire & malice and more of a headache than a hallelujah!!

So, what to do, huh? Get a job, work for myself—I also live in a state where I am wanted by the law—Instant jail the 1st time a Calif cop asks me for my ID—So, what? Move? Go to jail? Get a lawyer? Move out of state?—Why stay here? Why not?

Fish or cut bait or fish or cut bait or fish, etc…etc…
Can you see the confusion here?

So once again, sitting in a city park, a green belt, biospheric tonic of the city bound—black walnut trees dominate the skyline—why go to work? Someone has to "not go to work"—word games, sophistry—this is why people set up these parks, so a person can get away from their own personal urban/soap opera stress patterns—just a small break, mostly mental, mostly subjective—

I think I am on the way out, so to speak—I don't figure to be here, alive, all that much longer—10 years if I'm lucky, w/any kind of health—so how to use these years—what happens if I'm crippled before I die? Do I go on? Suicide? What to do, where, why to do it? 46 years old—mid-life crisis? Blathering? Real problems? Paranoia? Why now? So judge yourself by standards of perfection & wonder why you are found wanting by yourself, by your own impossible standards—I am not perfect, striving maybe but nowhere even close, not today!!

DEAD SCARED

People Are Dead Scared Of Kevorkian—

they ain't just wishing again
        there up in Michigan,

if you're tired of it
        party on out
                & say good-bye—

you & your buddies cut the cake
        blow out the candles
you're off to heaven
        they're off to jail—

if everybody just left you alone
        what would you do?
why, you'd just die—

3.10.94

Jan 1, 1994 am

Well, we not only have a new year, but a new diary for '94—of course it is recycled in the finest fashion of the third world, a past birthday present from Katie Brennan in/on xmas 1976/Cohasset in the whispering pines—

Katie is now 17 yrs older & has a steady named K.P. Brown, AKA Ken—they were here for New Year's day dinner; just another reason to get high—Ken & I are totally into smoking w/o the no-inhaling vibes; Katie inhales too, but she prefers to think otherwise; maybe she will grow up to be president, ol' Willie sure did—

So! 1994! Resolutions be damned—money is alright, why not that for a change?—guilt, not guilt; gain instead of pain; the brook instead of de Nile!

Just a note on 12 am New Years—enough gunfire to seem Somali-ish—where oh where is Mike Ramsey?!!

Jan 1 1994 pm

Work, responsibilities, possibilities, creativities, not so much into changes, just moving past the mental, the understanding—this is the year of the dynamic, the do-it, the "finally get it on"; at another milepost, another turn in the read—make it happen; front off the bullshit, get it out of the way!

January 9 1994 Libra/Scorpio
Happy birthday, Barb Derr
cool, cloudy→sunshine

Well, another day of working—pay the mortgage, killing time—cooking for little ol' ladies, staying poor but have beer in the fridge & the bills are paid—still looking for the perfect job—Clancy picked me up an application to Ceramics Lab at Butte College, who knows?? I need a good full time, or another good part-time job—want extra money for 4 cases of brewed beer— Gene up this weekend, hopefully enough cash to do something—if Mark comes through, fine, if not, I'm going to fuck with him big time, just for too many times irritated—

Jan 6 94
clear cold Scorpio moon

No rain—frost & almost ice, working evening shift, 2 day off following, sold 130.00 model airplanes to Don from work, pays car insurance for 3 mos, Ruthie gets a little extra—haven't had a smoke in 3 days—no big deal,

175

figure I saved 20.00, what an 1/8 cost & it lasts me about 3 days—beer consumption cut in ½, still probably too much—actually sleeping better, must be working harder than I thought—Well, actually now 6 hrs later—must admit that I just plain got fucked up & fucked off—oh, well, by the bye & bye, by the by & high!

It's a hard rain, it's a hard rain, it's a hard rains a gonna fall...of course I end the day pissed off, another screaming session w/my lil "nut & honey"—of all the things that I do, arguing w/Buttons is the most draining, negative thing, worse by far than drug addiction; with a good ol' addiction, stop doing the drug, no more problem; but this?

Jan 7 94
cold clear
another day
let's do it different

Up early, bored at 5 am, too cold & dark to go out yet—maybe build a workspace for clay & play—find a propane tank & regulator for the stove, some roofing & I'm in business—
Sat., all set, I think, a done deal; maybe; Mark!—

Jan 9 94
cool foggy rainy wet

So Sun am early, go to work in a few minutes, coffee cake & poached eggs, yummy—So, Saturday! Mark is a 1st class asshole! 5 hours late, but was properly apologetic & humble, still what a jerk—enough recompense to make up for, just resent wasting ½ day on his account—did go to work; came home; some good beer & very excellent smoke & company, Conner & family, car work, the 110.00 gone like only yesterday can—the house is fairly shouting neglect, drip drip creak creak

Mon am 10 Jan
Cold, clear

Up too early, 2 am, not tired, just couldn't sleep—so just spacing, getting ready for work, paperwork & old movies, waiting for the E.R.—

Fri am 1.14.94
cold clear fog Aquarius/Pisces

So, tues wens workdays, clear cold, etc, thurs a day off, did not much of
nothing, today so far is a start of a repeat—2 am shifts coming up w/a
Cohasset party Sunday night, bed & breakfast & back to work—payday
came & went; little money left over, but the bills are paid, etc...job cut-off
date now Feb 12—pays the mortgage again and still another job out there
just waiting for me—

Sat 5 am 1.15.94
Aries moon
clear cool

And I ended yesterday by going to bed—This morning started when I got
up—Buttons up at 4 am, 3-day week-end, early start

Sun 1.16.94
cold clear

Up early, Buttons w/Nancy—go to work in an hour—RB & potatoes, mock
Napoleons, anniversary dinner/party at Clancy & Susan's tonight—spend
the night & go to work 11 am Monday—car being fixed—cost 300.00+, in
last week, still needs brake job, etc...

Thur 1.20
5 pm clear
Taurus moon

So, go to work in some kind of shape mon morn, Dan home sick, busy—tues
called in early/wens & thurs work—fri I'm off—weather is beautiful...the
party Sunday was mellow/drunk, good country hippie vibes—Conner is very
much people oriented, very centered—Patrick is too cute sometimes,
obnoxious even—oh well, Clancy's friend, not mine; Susan put on a nice job
as hostess—her day calls 4:30 am w/LA quake news, Tris calls Wens eve,
chit chat, it's cold in PA.

Sun 23 Jan 94
rain finally, Gemini moon/Leo
So, it's finally raining, not much of a storm, but it is the 1st of the year—
work, etc...Friday off, smoked the last and there was none—2 wks of

quantity & quality + free, who is to complain?—watching early morning
t.v.—"Buns of steel" w/Tammy Lee, old movies, "To Hell W/the Blonde
Blaspheming Bombshell" or something—if it wasn't so early I'd be bored—

24 Jan 94
rainy cool cold
Leo moon

So, another day of winter, the 2nd of this year, or actually the 4th or 5th, but
the 2nd in 2-3 weeks—pissed off about the check book, Buttons & her give-
a-fuck attitude about it—well, it's all the same old bullshit, but I'm not used
to it after all this time, what's to give a fuck!

27 Jan 94 Leo/Virgo
clear cold

So, it's another new day, looking at the last couple, then forward towards
today & even for the next month—lots of changes starting w/Ruthie moving
in, Mar 1; whole house going through spring cleaning a season early—I'm
looking for another job, again—3 more weeks at the Care West & then sub
time & a new job—

Jan 30 Virgo Moon
cold clear 6 am

So, it's mostly work, plus a house trip, bills are getting paid, alcohol is the
only big money drain, 300+ a month for the 2 of us, not counting smokes—
stupid sort of behavior, isn't it? Oh well, call me stupid—K.T. bought a
small ho-made trailer, heading for the woods of upper Michigan, should be
interesting—Chuck has a new girl friend, could Squeak & Damien be
coming back to Chico?

Feb 3 94
Virgo/Scorpio
light fog

Another day at work—8 more at Care West, another job search, looking for
a payday!

FOOLISH

Priests turn out
    to be perverts—

Medicine men talk fools
    into donning ghost shirts,
said the bullets would pass right thru 'em
    & out the other side—
just ask a dead buffalo
    if that wasn't so—

You think maybe
    someone could of figured
        all this out,
But, no! Warriors or not, courage put aside,
    we are talking foolish here—

3.27.94

□□□

DOMINION THEREOVER

Where do we want the whales,
    dead, alive, endangered?
When they were ignored
    no on paid attention,
even burning in lamps
    their very essence
flickered,
    the light shed on bibles
& verses of dominion thereover—

(Dominion thereover—ask a buffalo
if that ain't so)

4.4.94

FRACTALS

Fractals,
   what
      every pot smoker
has seen
   but can't articulate,
but so what,
it took the rest
   of the straight world
   until this decade
to discover it
     their
        own selves

4.25.94

☐☐☐

MISSING THE POINT

Someone is missing the point!

Patterns, order, chaos, Santana
   fractal imaginations
order
   out of the chaos
of brown & white
   Latin & hip-hop
spirit & the flesh
   youth answers to age
insistent solid beat, cooperative rhythm
   harmony tossed into the chaos

BALANCE

See there, a dog
   with a bad hind leg
uses balance for a crutch
   a leaf falls thoughtlessly—

     □□□

BALLS

I knew nuns who
   were as crazy
as Joan of Arc
   they just didn't have
the balls to go to war—

     □□□

BEAST

Tame the beast?
   The hell! you say,
cloak the
   appetite
in symbols,
   and
let him
   rage
      on—

5.15.94

SHAMEFUL CREATURE

People in China,
    dicks dragon in the dirt
        so to speak,
eat the horns of rhinos,
        cocks of tiger,
    bear pizzles,
suck the scrotums
        of massive bulls,
    proud of their rutting—
Man is such a shameful creature!

            4.4.94

□□□

DANCING WITH CHAOS

Just because
    chaos
dances w/us all
    doesn't mean
she's fickle

            4.25.94

□□□

MORE OR LESS

Much more
    than a
        Haiku
A bit less
    than a Koan
Sometimes a
    kick in the ass
        tho
a bit less than
    a caning

            5.22.94

JETSOM & FLOTSAM

The "videos", the "videos"
    like the "power poles"
the "power poles"
        Carlos waving his arms
                as he exclaims—
        lights flashing
                digital sound tracks
        descroo—descroo—descroo
                Jack Kerouac
        ocean hysterical raving
                noise
        so oo has crash beep beep beep
crash crumble skoosh scrash oom
        finally this jetsom
                flotsam
        after all this time
                on its currents
        washed ashore
                co-interested now—bones
in with the bits of Styrofoam & shells
        dead bodies of mammals

                1994→1995

HARSH TINKLE

God is everywhere...

In a sense
           of humor
        perhaps
he thinks it funny:

Nov 65
the Ham Luong river,
        gunboats & grenades,
50 rangers killed & wounded
        when grenades carried
by a fellow ranger
        exploded and all
aboard this
        totally armoured
tin can
        were caught in the
harsh tinkle
        of god's sweet laughter—

                        5.4.94

                □□□

GOD WOULD

And god
        Would do that!

And cause that contrast
        between that holy communion
        of souls
and that splendid isolation
        that is the free will—

                        July 17, 96

BUDDHA & BUTTONS
I-CHING COINS

Casting
    about
to write about,
    wanting to write
a poem
    about whatever—
I was going
    to ask you
but
    what it came to
was
    your I-Ching
coins;
    for casting about
that's quite a coincidence—

Chuck 5.28.94

19 Aug 95—getting used to
hot & humid & ho hum

Dear Linda—

Hello, how are you? I am fine! Hope you are too! I am so lonely now
in my life—listening to Tom Rush:

> "We would only cry again,
> say goodbye again—"

> "Strange faces
> in your place
> can't keep the ghosts away—"

> "No regrets, no tears goodbye,
> don't want you back,
> we'd only cry again,
> say goodbye again—"

This is one of those songs that always reminds me of you, brings up
every memory of you—listening to 101 FM, the River FM—hot, humid
Illinois listen-to-the-radio night—

Wens 2 Aug 95—Illinois
rain humid so—ho—hum

2 weeks into this trip—Cal→Ill. again
19 July Chico→Winnemuca—3 am, sitting up scratching notes & nursing a
beer—finally get a motel & sleep a few hours—next to south of Salt Lake—
all day sick as two dogs hung-over—motel early, not well at all—

Damien of course has been here all along; this, an entire 'nother
story—
So the next day, 21 July, we are off into So. E. Utah & into Colo→
Kansas—600 mi, up & down, round & round switch-back city, at the
bragged about 80 mph average since Nevada—I thought the g-forces were
some form of hang-over, but we really moved right along—we stop just w.
of Kansas—that becomes tomorrow.

So, thunderstorms all across E. Colo. lightning, black clouds, hail, wind, Welcome home C.B.

Up fairly early Colo. time, off we go—Mo. bound, cross over at K.C. by mid day, stop early, get into Luke's early Sun morn. First off, no one gets into a motel on a Friday, sat eve w/o reservations, every motel for 50 mi into Mo. is booked all summer—imagine that! River casinos, holidays/Branson right down the road. So we go to Po-dunk , Mo and sure enough find that sort of motel—

But we are now up early again, that much closer to my brother's place—we make it by 9:30 or so—great drive, except—have I mentioned the thunderstorms again or not, the lightening for the 1st time this whole trip we begin to see accidents, gnarly scenes w/semi's & dead babies—just kidding

So Sun→Mon/Alan's→tues→to Mo again—decal a trailer for United Vans $50 to Damien, likewise to myself—

Wens 1st week out—run Leroi down—go see Randy, same BS as last time—put in for a couple of jobs—Paul, my nephew, has a birthday party— Buttons calls, a most rational sort of call—

—lunch with my mom, dinner at home, meet a few old friends, meet a few new ones, get a job on Friday, don't have to start until Monday, great—a Calif style deli-restaurant—no money but right downtown, all 3 blocks of it—Edwardsville is the Madison County seat, w/a pop. of 14,000—there is an Ill. Univ. on the edge of town, with an enrollment of 11,000 but it is a commuter college, & none of them live in town—

Sun—we go back to Missouri, a mini-family reunion out at Luke's, my aunt, Sister Bede is there along with my mom, two of the most Catholic women I could think of; well, except for maybe the rest of them—strange way of looking at life—God is a reality here, you have to accommodate him—so we have this BBQ—my sister-in-law wants me to "get my shit together", along w/a hair cut; my aunt, sister Bede, a nun, prays for me & my mom owes me 10 bucks—Damien lays plans here to jump ship to Luke's for the week—two to one he pulls the same stunt that he did in Chico & heads back to Calif—

So—that's kind of part of Sunday—Sunday night, Alan emotes, as he can & then some—great, my nutty little brother—

Monday, 31 July, I go back to work—likewise tues & wens, which is the same wens as today, my time—

15 August
moon in the sky

Well, Stagger Inn again; staggered in, been staggering since—people are just too fucking intense—boredom, just energy spinning its wheels—round & round in gear, out of gear—transmission slipping, no neutral but what gravity gives you—I have been here before, but I really can't tell where this is at all—

So, I'm almost a month into this chapter of my life—I had more fun than a Budapest Circus family—I am a two-headed geek, I am a bearded dog-faced boy, I am the void in between meaningful spaces—I have created spaces, vacuums that beg to be filled—I am creating blank, white spaces that draw images—

Today, right now, a continuation of last night—totally spatial, temporal disorientation, part of it all, Jerry Garcia died—nothing tragic, he just died—

So, today is part of last night—a few hours sleep & the dream continues—why I think that this activation of consciousness is reality is just another problem to work through—

My dreams never infringe on reality—well, almost never—in 20 years, I've dreamt of Buttons 2-3 times; always those dreams are part of not sleeping that semi-conscious state, usually associated w/abuse—skip the body around, wonder why this stimulation—

Listening to music, John Prine & how he sees the world—wonder why I have to …why I can't hear it—it does force a person to pay attention to the nuances, to appreciate the subtleties…

…so this is dissolving into gibberish, the light is bad, I am still drunk, more than drunk, brain dead—

17 August air conditioned
unpacked, filling in
the spaces, pushing up
to edges

Sitting here unpacked & cluttering it up again—nothing on this wall here yet;
so I think so, being out of tacks; so I look up, I have an ant, active actually,
he was here at the beginning of this, now to be somewhere else, took a
minute so to speak to track & register—a largish black ant on a pure new
white wall—

      Long winded haiku—so to speak, the longest title to a non-
existent poem, there is something here in Illinois that grabs your attention,
thunderstorms neg-pos, limestone fossils, part of this thought comes from
dreams of dead Indians, part subjectivity, Melissa Etheridge, a memory of
MTV, glances & insinuations

NEARING CENTER

My life at this time
    has become nearing center
        because of this place—
the center
    the anchor of this occilation
steadrock refusal
    to give way to that tension
    releasing to chaos
cohesion cheated actually

there is a part of poetry
    that begs the eyes,
that godly interruption
    of life to the mind
that scorns the symphony
    of speech
& demands the regions
    of thought
to judge a reality—

Aug 19 same o same o
going to go dancing
in a lesbian bar

Stagger In again & again—BS Gemini day—twins Ping & Pong all day—

Met a guy from the Netherlands—told him that the Stagger, as an extension of America, was basically a soap opera—it got his interest, he even said so—the pulse & vibes of the place was then expounded on—his name was Camille, he was sitting w/an international set of friends, all of them upper college level; one lady from France, totally bald, totally proud bone structure—

All I've done since I've been here is meet people—all of these people just waiting & waiting to be met—I feel like John Muir in Yosemite Valley, Boaz the old anthropologist w/the Indians—making more mistakes than friends—but then I am choosy—and as Gracie Slick says, "It don't mean shit to a tree", which probably brought a laugh out of John—

So, life has been pretty strange lately—not so much strange as it is interesting; not so much fun but it is interesting—

I'm working part-time, looking for another job, or more hours, or a part-time etc...

I have a new place, but only make enough money to survive—I'm renting off Vern Carver, a face from the early 70's, one of Gene's ex-partners—nice place almost cheap, for being in town, it's kind of in the country; actually it is very similar to Gettysburg—small town almost to a soap opera, but I have been here before, so it is not too strange—

My current patron this trip is a very old time brother-buddy, name of Leroy Valentine Moody—another German-Czech-gypsy—we share history, family & friends, past adventures
Sept 5 cooler, sunny
getting bogged down here

25 September

Just a thought—there was a religion in China & the Orient, the Jan's—one of their basic beliefs was that all life is equal, that man & ants were partners

& buddies in life's little dance of the molecules—so, to be nice they would sweep the paths as they walked along—so that any ants & their little bug friends would not be stepped on, would not be sent back intothat void, the molecule pot, for yet another restructuring—

The thought was—a broom & the stiff bristles taller than redwoods, massive to the ants, thought is was like being killed by friendly fire—a B-52 strike on a trench full of Iraqis is off by just a bit, multiply by 8 miles high & those tons of explosives are in your life & it's back to the molecules—

So, I'm broke all the way to death—it is beer or bills—kind of a problem where if I do pay the bills, I won't have enough money to drink, if I do drink I won't have a place to drink—I should do something about this I guess but today is just beginning, I do have a beer & I'm drinking it in my own house, so I guess this problem still has a way to go before the crossroad—

Crossroad, as a concept—you come to me, your choices are to the right, to the left, on ahead, stop & go back—such a simple thing, a crossroad, only a few simple choices, but the what & where of your life becomes something you can't foresee, you just have to go & do it—actually you could just stand there forever, talk to people as they pass through & on, but you could also drown in a rainstorm, another dumb turkey

So, I finally write to buttons—haven't mailed it yet, but I will; I just do that, write letters & then wait weeks to mail em—I'm kind of lazy, kind of an ass—this is part of my life that didn't go away just because I went away—can "getting a life" actually still have one, a life in the past that is still a present reality—

1 Oct 95 full moon soon
warm to cool, trees
beginning to change

So—her name is cocaine—fell off the wagon with a 'bump' as they say around here—not so much of a jar when I fell off but it is probably on its way—
Bogus trip from the get go—a Sears poncho as Frank was apt to say—
First, ol' Leroy comes by, wants to know if I want to go to a party—
I'm for it, why not, Saturday is not only payday, but it is my Friday night—
met some new people, see a bunch from the Stagger, great food, free beer—

191

had a conversation w/a lady named Ann—met her dad, listened to her husband play guitar—she was in the kitchen when I met her, she washes dishes for her friends at their parties—asked if she was maybe a c
Cancer, nope, a Leo—later, outside, it's getting dark, she talks way low register, I actually hear maybe half of what she says, she tells me that a while ago she was raped & how this trauma changed her—she lives w/burglar alarms & paranoid caution—her mind was pushed enough so that she imagines her own future & causes most of it to happen—Marcus Aurelius said something like this—everyone knows the end of the story—

I talk to Dave, Matt's dad—Matt was four yrs old today—in two weeks he goes in for major reconstructive surgery for bone strangeness around his face & skull—this is one tough kid—

So we leave, Leroy to his office, me to home—but I go down to the Stagger Inn again—Mike the anthropologist introduces me to Andy, drunk & from Chicago, found his maybe girlfriend in bed w/someone—the bar fills up, strange brew tonite—the old crowd at the party—the bar scene becomes crowded w/strange faces—and a few from the past, again

Oct 7 full moon rising
coolish, lots of strange

So, her name is Buttons—she's my wife, the second one—she's going to come to Illinois in a month or so, a very major change in things that I have been creating as current—the last few days have been very high energy concepts in almost all of the phases of my life—
My job vibes have been strange—the downtown deli has been weird w/new owners, everything out of sync. When Jane left, so did the bracing from the infrastructure—I get an interview for another job, one of the rivals down the street, this time of calling, time of interviewing comes in the middle of all this strangeness—
I have a couple of advancements towards my own business—food to compete w/the downtown people—my thoughts coincide w/others/strange

COURAGE

they faced cannon
    & musket
w/only honor & courage

are people so
    in love
      w/death?
they chase after it,
    they would
        run it to the ground
like a fox in the hunt

they stand up
    & demand it
for themselves & others
    as if it were a privilege
a grand favor given
    an honor bestowed

they have the courage
    to demand it—

Buttons & Pick-up & Dog & Beer, Time & Place Unknown

INTO ILLINOIS

So, her name is Buttons, my wife
      Marion Roberta Owen-Luetkemeyer
& she was in my thoughts today
            & my conversations
            & then she was outside of Salt Lake City
      & we talked of going up & onto
            the high plain country
                  of Wyoming
into Nebraska
      several different routes
            south, south east
      on into Mo, Mighty Mo
& then onto, into Illlinois—

1996

194

NOTES TO AND FROM BUTTONS
FROM JOURNAL DATED OCT 16.95→OCT 96

16 Oct Mom's B.day
cool clear windy

Dear Buttons,

Hello, sweetheart of mine! Miss you something terrible, will be good
to see you again.

Well, work is interesting—the Dew Drop Inn Café—work part is
fairly easy, but when they get busy, it is busy—but there are lots of lulls—
some of the food is pretty good, lots of specials, homecooked this and that—
it's nothing too good, but not too bad—typical home cooking, greasy
spoon—every old geezer in town comes in—I serve as many sides of jello as
I do French fries—oatmeal for breakfast, or biscuits & gravy forever—it's
an old kitchen but not too dirty—Theresa is a real slave driver, but she isn't
an asshole about it; not always anyway…

Buttons—
I am cashing a check at the Dew Drop—if you need gas money come
on by, early if you want to miss Mother T—
                                        See ya,
                                        Chuck
B—
Skip the shaving cream, I'm growing a beard.

                          C—
Chuck—
I love you, I'm sorry
Let's not fuck it up this time
                    B
B—
Too cheap to buy a card
        no flowers, no candy
But hey, what the heck
you want to say you're sorry
        I think you're sorry—

                    Chuck

Buttons,

    I went to bed at 8:15, so if I'm still in bed at 4-4:30, don't worry about waking me—

                See ya,
                    Chuck
                        Any mail?

B—

Good morning my little sweet thing, my little slice of pound cake w/cool whip, love of my life, etc...

    Hi—the rent check is in your check book—that's all

                            I love you
                              Chuck

If it's not raining, could you put the green bike in the car—thanks
                                  call me

Buttons,

    Couldn't find the checkbook to enter my checks—any ideas?
See you at 1:30 or so—

    Get me some beer if you go to store—also toilet paper
                        Love you
                        Chuck

THE FOLLOWING: dates unknown, possibly SECRET HARBOR, WASHINGTON

Buttons—

    Good morning my little waffle #3 w/strawberries & cool whip, hope your morning is sunny-side up or at least OE. If you go to de sto, get me some beer—

                I'm a jerk
                & off to work
                    Chuck—

Chuck, good morning, I love you.
                Buttons

Buttons,
    good morning—

the video was worth watching

Rich might be by 10ish to pick up the sleeping bag—it won't bother me if you get into the closet to get it—

Have a good one—don't forget the boxes in the trunk—

good night,

Chuck

Chuck,

went to bed at 11 am…get up whenever?

I love you

B

PS Rich brought some stuff by this am—tell you about it later

Buttons—

B—

Good morning & good night

Set the alarm for 2:30 am—you can leave it on the table if the door is open—see you at 1:30 or so Sun

I love you

Chuck

Chuck,

good morning you 2 AM person! This is too weird. Have a nice day, night, afternoon?

Love, B

Buttons,

K.T. didn't know the hosp. address, she will find out today—she wants you to call her—

thanks,

Lord love a Chuck

Buttons,

If you go out, could you drop this off at the library for me, it's due, thanks

Chuck

Chuck,
    if you'd like to go to V.I. for a drink when I get off—It's a possibility!
Maybe a burger or FF?
        Love, B
        Theron was supposed to be fired last night. I'd love to gloat.

Buttons—
    Call Leroy, Gene & Leslie, K.T. (1/8 pot)
                C

B—
    good morning my little cupcake, my ding-dong
        I'm a jerk who went to...
            See you at 1:10 or so
           Love you
              C—
           would appreciate a beer if you go by the
           store
B—
    Good morning, lucky you, stay-at-home baby—
        My check will be late today, so why not pick me & the check
up at 1:30ish and we can do lunch somewhere—
           Call me if you are into it
            Chuck

Buttons,
    left my beer in the car, can you leave it here for me—thanks
                C—

B—
    if I'm sleeping call me in sick—
    Peggy will only be there from 7-8 am
    I have never felt this bad, not even going cold turkey
              C—

B—
    Good morning my little Cupcake
        Sorry I was such an ass last nite
           C—

B—

      made you some crackers—also check out the stamp drawer in the
desk

                C—

B—

      if you get some yeast & flour & oil I'll make some bread this
afternoon—

            C

Poopsie!

      There's beer in the fridge & a gram on order from Joan
             See you around 7:30
                  Love,
                    B

B—

      Good morning my little angle
      I know it's misspelled
      but it does rhyme
          w/dangle—
      Just found the pipe and the ashtray
      in the garbage—am I high?
             Love you
               C—

B—

      Well, baby, this is it, I'm out the door
          I'll try to call this evening just to say goodnight.
                  I love you,
                  C—
      B.S would love you forever if you'd
      save me another perko—
      of course I'll love you
         forever
            anyway
      see ya fri nite

Buttons,,
    Good morning,
        Glad we're friends again—I put baking soda on the dog piss
        You might wander on it
            or even vacuum—
        that was my list for you today
        I will have another $15.00 this afternoon—I spent 3.00 on
pizza & 30.00 on pot—enjoy
    It was a long day—Happy fri nite
                      C—

B—
        the laundry bag is in a black bag on the yellow chair if you want to
add to it—
    A shower curtain would be nice; of course a bath is nice, too!
    Hung over like a M.F.
    We could use a really good box if you spot one anywhere; like a
produce, Z wall, Zbox-box—a duffel bag would be good, too—
        Well baby hi ho hi ho, etc…
                      C—

Buttons—
    Good morning—
        don't forget to turn off the heat when you leave
        I took 8.00, left you 20.00
        are we broke yet?
            Love & kisses
                to my little mrs!
        What the fuck? it rhymes
                Chuck

B—
    Good morning my precious
    just thought I'd tell you that I love you—
    It's 4 am & I'm a jerk to work, etc…
    I think Butch & Joan are having lunch w/us, so if you would finish off
the stew, that would be nice—I'll be hungry; just doing my share—
    Well, off I go, hi ho, hi ho
        I stink, therefore
        I am
            Chuck

Buttons,

    good morning my precious, just a warm wake-up note—sorry for not cleaning up the mess but I didn't want to make a lot of noise—

    There is a La Crème container full of meat scraps for trachor in the fridge, I didn't feed him—should be used before it spoils—

                Well, off to work—see ya
                   Chuck

    I love you—last nite was a little kinky, but still, great, great sex—hope you are not as sore as I am, my "pretty gymnast" & fuck the neighbors if they can't take a joke, right?

Chuck!

    Look in the letter from Leroy. Haven't gotten the money from Butch & Joan yet. They're looking for pot, but haven't found any yet. KT started her new job today at some restaurant down by the ferry. She should be home some time around 3 pm. If you have time watch the movie on the desk. It's highly amusing. It doesn't have to be turned in until 5 pm.

                See you at 6.
                Love,
                  B

Chuck,

    well—the hospital called last night & I have to work the C-2 shift tomorrow—Julia is sick—so don't wake me up. I'm not going in till 9:30—boo hoo!

          Love,
            B

B—

    Good morning—sorry about the schedule change, I missed you—call you 8:30ish
    Chuck

B—

    Well, there isn't any more hope
        of getting any more dope
    and I still gotta do another show
        door—

Don't worry about my grey pants & shirt, I'm wearing them
See you this pm
Love you
Chuck

B—

Went up to the little park up the road—W. Park
if anyone calls, tell 'em I'm sleeping & I'll call back 3 – 4
see you around 1 or so
C—

B—

good morning—
I put the money in your purse—if you go to Payless, pick-up that
present for Cindy for me please or something 10.00ish—thanks
C—

B—

went to bed, I'll get up if I hear you—no go w/Dan, didn't talk to
Joan—his money in my wallet
love you
C—

Chuck,

I called & talked to Linda—Tris wants you to call her!
B

Buttons,

leave the scissors out so I can trim my mustache—thanks
C—

B—

I watched the video up to same place you did—don't watch the rest
w/o me
C—

Chuck,

just dropped this off so you wouldn't have to wait all day
Love,
B—save me some!

B—

    One good bud deserves another
                        C—

B—

    this one can be used anyday including fri & sat
    just leave my pot on the desk, I have a lighter—
                        C—

B—

    there is a roast in icebox for sandwiches or whatever—asparagus &
tomato on bottom shelf—rolls on counter—save me the corn—
                thanks
                    C—

Don't forget to leave my pot on your desk—papers in the rolling bowl—
again, thanks

B—

    So, I'm the giant asshole for eating <u>your</u> port cutlet—you bought it, I
ate it, I suck—
    So, then you fuck up a pork cutlet, eat ½ of another—
    So, you have a sandwich on bread I bought, w/a tomato I bought,
finish that off with a ¼ of an apple pie, maybe some ice cream, wipe your
mouth w/some paper towels & wipe your ass 2/t.p. you didn't buy—
    So, I'm an asshole who ate your pork cutlet—
    So, food for thought—who bought that, huh? Why don't you go fuck
yourself & do it today
                C—

Chuck
    RE: The great TV dinner blowout…
    I'm sorry if I offended you. Can't we just put a little perspective on
this and leave it where it belongs? Over.
    Happy St. Paddy's day
        Later…B
        (You can have my shells if you want)

B—

give me the rent schedule for above months—make sure the landlady has the same schedule—please do this afternoon so I can write it into my calendar

thank you,

or else!

C—

B—

Boo is in back yard—she is mad at me, something to do with a water-machine gun, really bums her out—
Damien is supposed to call; find out if & when he is coming down—
Don't give any pork bones to Boo, she is stuffed, fed her at noon—
What is happening w/Vito & the kid's b-day party—can Tris & Damien go? What time, etc…? Any smoke anywhere?

See ya,

C—

PERSONAL CHEF

If you are a busy professional or just too busy to take the time to prepare delicious, nutritious meals, call Chuck & Buttons. We are just waiting to hear from you. Together, we have over 50 years experience with preparing any type of menu. We can cook from your menu or present you with one to fit your needs. Call for details…

Grandma Chuck's
Homestyle Cooking In Your Home

C B Luetkemeyer
Personal Cook

1264 E 10th St
Chico, Ca
95929
Phone: 530-342-6586

E-mail: nonamechuc@aol.com

Geraldine, can you make this sound better? (vegetarian, ethnic, diabetic, lowfat)

Buttons

C—

Don't forget the boxes! Excellent movie on the video if you can get past the 1st 15 minutes. It's well worth watching. Keep the roast in the pan— I'm going to use the drippings.

B—

B—

Hope this is enough—would you make all the burger up into burgers (fried) & I'll eat this evening—you can have some too—

See ya

C—

B—

Just a small list of things to do
    on your day off—
Get up when you want,
stay in your P.J.s till
you want to get dressed,
have a cigarette or two,
maybe a drink,
eat when you want
let the cat & dog in & out
    & in & out & in.
Watch T.V.,
maybe have another cig
    & something to eat
or another drink—
Don't forget to let the cat & dog
    in & out & in & out—
Don't answer the phone, it's
probably me with more
things to do—
Don't forget that I love you,

    Chuck—

Remember that the cat & dog
    need that old in & out & in...

205

AND THAT WAS
THE HONYAK HOTEL

This story, because you have to,
          has a dragon—
and maidens & madness
    men of stout good nature
elves & fairies
          a troll
    mostly of good nature
              but so more sensitive
    to the poisons always
    to the fences & walls
          the gates & portals
    of the Honyak Hotel
and tho all of these and more
    were there, really there
some are lies on their way
          to a good story
and then some we make up

5.25.96

3.9.96 Scorpio moon
Edwardsville, Illinois

So, her name is still [xxx]
        and now her name
                has meaning—

Six months ago
        was just a glimpse
an intimation
        of yesterday
and now today
        and then tomorrow—

Another verse, another line
        in the Stagger Inn Blues
                again—

Illinois, winter Illinois
        cold, grey,
closed in, locked,
        cabin fever isolation,
the crowd becomes self—

So, her name is still [xxx],
        more so now than then,
before a wanting
        giving way to illusion,
giving way to form,
        to a reality
that cost all of the illusion—

And then a phone call:
        "I need to talk to you"
        "No, you don't"

So, her name is still [xxx]
        & I need to talk about her—

                4.15.96

GOD BLESS THE WOMENS!

So, her name was Clair Francis
Yarsinski
    & she was my mother!

And she was the first woman
that I have ever known—(born 12.25.46)

And then her name was
        Pat
    Patricia Ann Luetkemeyer
So, she was my oldest sister
    and already there—(born 11.44)

Of course & no doubt
             doubtless
there was a nurse
    nurses more than just her
but in that instant
        that shattering
    aware blinding instant
I failed to notice, unaware

and my mother's mother
    and my father's mother
had all these children
    these then
        my aunts & uncles
            cousins
        nieces, nephews
    some here then
        now
            later
and all thes
    great & grand of my mother
        and father

but this mostly
    a story
of all the womens—

If this were the weaving
        of some sort of tale
a tapestry, the fabric,
then the men will be the knots
held together & the women will be the tale

4.16.96 Aries moon
spring hope & perhaps

Winter started early
        1995
about the time when
    Jerry Garcia dies
& the keep on trucking
    vitamin c &
you just knew
    that if you got home
    before daylight you must
    might get some sleep tonite—

but you never did—

And everybody seemed
    To be tiring
the heat of last summer
        almost—

So, her name is Pattie & her mother is dying—her pain tears at me,
her rage at the comprehension of it all shames me—and the beast won't go
to sleep

    and the moon's too bright
        and the chains are too tight
            and the beast won't go to sleep

[MISCELLANEOUS THOUGHTS ON POST-IT NOTES, APRIL 1996]

• Two parts of the conversation got through to this level—I'm hearing, one sided of course, he says, "The cook just quit" My name is Chuck; Chuck just quit—then, because a sense of humor is the only coin, he says, "The key?"... pause..."yeah, he stuck it in my croissant!"

• Opinions, we trade them amongst ourselves like kid's comics & baseball cards

• Just woke up...dreamt I was washing this huge brown rabbit—it was loving it & kept drinking the water—the alarm goes off—foggy headed & thirsty as hell, I'm up; it must have been a wet dream—

• "And where were you when the shit hit the fan?" "Standing directly behind it" said the lunatic with the shovel—

• A solution akin to giving your 120 lb pit bull methamphetamine to cure rabies—a bad idea that is only going to be getting worse as time goes by—

• Once you take that leap off the high board, it is a little silly to worry if there is any water in the pool—

5.8.96
Edwardsville, Illinois

If I didn't have a sense of humor, I wouldn't have any sense at all—

So, her name is [xxx]—this makes the evening interesting—some people jump out of airplanes; some people play with snakes & vipers so deadly in their consequences that God sits ever so lightly on their shoulders, not even a smile to wear down this sensitivity—[xxx] is my girlfriend, tho this story is mostly more than "another woman" story—Last nite was the 1st time in months that I talked to her face to face—the last time was a black winter storm sunrise & it was very physical & I counted backwards from 20, I told her she would come before I counted out to zero—she screamed no, she screamed no, & when I said 6 & then 4, she screamed & screamed—

When Buttons & I split up last March, she told me she was moving in w/[xxx] to wait out a few days of taking care of business before heading back to Calif—I was not of sound mind that weekend, & I told both [xxx] & Buttons what truth was all about—so I lost my wife, lost my girlfriend, everything but my sense of humor—

And last nite I looked into her eyes & I was real to her again—she is still very angry but she looked into my eyes & we were real again, to each other—she left & I sat there for awhile & for awhile till closing—I left a ¼ oz & a 12 pack in Leroy's car—I came home, don't know if I walked or someone gave me a ride—

So, her name was [xxx], last July '95, my 1st day in Illinois this time—Leroy introduces me to her—I talk to her for a couple hours—I call her at 2-3 am next morning—tell her good night—her boyfriend is a real jerk about it—but he is [not here] & I made very serious physical love to [xxx]— then I lost it all—

Every once in a while, Leroy comes by—always a cultural experience—we have a few beers, cut a few lines, count up the coins & out the door—Yesterday—a new Stones CD, going to Hamel to find a key— talking about this & that: the 60's & hiway 66—Vietnam, Cambodia, Kent State & Ho Chi Minh in Paris—his cousin, Kurt, was not home, but talk to the kids, his grandma, drink a few beers, she is 88, but a Checho, not a Slovakian—she sits at sewing machine, cloth in one hand, beer in the other, conversation, stitching, humming along—And then Ernie's, then Pontoon Beach, then Granite City & then Edwardsville & the Stagger—

By the time I hit the Stagger, I'm down to 40 bucks, have a happy face transdermal sort of on my shoulder—I run into [xxx]—God sits on my shoulder sometimes, he spurns televisions, his soap operas are not Sears soap operas—and when the time had come for the shit to hit the fan, the lunatic grabbed a shovel, turned the fan on high and went about it with gusto & enthusiasm—as the Chinese are fond of saying, It was interesting! My odds of dying from gun shot wounds from some jealous fool go up daily—the odds way better than the lottery and you don't need to buy a ticket—this for a woman whose last name is [xxx]; there was never a moment when I didn't know what would finally happen—her name has that call of dark magic; she, very aware of that powerful name, whispers promises that are dares & challenges—

Oh, well, sure beats watching television! Especially if you don't have one, anyhow—

5.9.96 Aquarius moon
mostly clear, warm

So, this is the 2nd day off from work, one day is to kick out the jams, the next to savor, succor & survive—to sit & sift through all those spilled grains of sand—go through all the pockets & cubbyholes, see what is what—

So this morning: 18.00, mostly ones & an ATM debit receipt for 110.00—a heroine transdermal analgesic stick-on patch—a coaster from Ernie's, a bar in Hamel on Rte. 66, of the old 66 legend, coast to Chicago, Jack Kerouac & hitchhike/backpack—a phone # from a 46 year old Sag. lady, a Harley shirt, high black boots, black leotards—she was Slovakian, as opposed to Chech-slo—Leroy is Chech, me & the lady Slovakian—all of us with German fathers—this in a bar in Granite City—all the folks are tattooed, looking like they should be on professional wrestling circuit—even the old lady type Illinois grey hairs have tattoos—she went to St. Teresa's in E. St. Louis—

8 Sept '96
58° at 6 am
full moon, harvest moon

So, this morning I'm treated to grey skies, cold grey misty rain – a 7 am walk down E. Union St, cutting over to Main, Rusty's around the corner from my trailer—the weather finally gave way to Autumn; the walk is brick streets—dags barking from behind tall wood fences—all up & down Union St; old houses, not so prosperous then or now, still sit just up from the narrow sidewalk; the plant life domesticated being crowded, pushed by the Illinois woods this time of the morning, only a small matter of yard cutting neglect and the weeds will have their way—

So, her name is [yyy]—she has already crowded my mind with memories, images & imaginations—There is a full moon rising, a harvest moon, let's go dancing in the light—

9 Sept '96
cool grey no wind
not as fall as yesterday am

So, the very act of going to bed with a woman, the talking & touching part, the waking up with this woman, or watching her sleep, this basic recipe is truly the bread of life—but sex makes it into a sandwich, it's the peanut butter & jelly, it's the BLT—so far, it's mostly bread, a lot of sandwiches w/o everything, just plain—

And now it is evening, a long sort of day—waiting, for?? Lonely is what lonely is—but I am wanting sleep in my own bed—I'm tired, this is my house—

16 Sept '96 early am
raining for a few hours

So, I end up in the Stagger for an hour or so—run into both [xxx] & [yyy]—chit-chatting like two sisters under the covers—didn't even know it was [yyy] till Leroy tells me—was talking to [xxx] for a while, her boyfriend giving me dirty looks from the end of the bar—fuck the spode in his ear—if he wants to keep something on a leash he should buy a dog—

So, next I'm talking w/[yyy], who is glad to see me & wants to know why I'm a stranger lately; I tell her I'm no stranger than usual—She is going to Ann's for take-out & headed home—I bum a ride to my trailer—she walks me down to my place & we sit & talk a while—of course I walk her back to her car—later, I call her to say goodnight—

18 Sept cooler, clear
Monday morning afterwards

So, I went to the Stagger Inn, again, again—had a whole house full of people but they were all watching the tube so Leroy & I walked on down the hall, to my extension of the living room, which is the Stagger—

[yyy] was there—Lauri was there w/her two dogs—a lot of people were there but mostly it was [yyy]—I offered once again to take her beau out back & stuff him in a garbage bin, but she tells me to be cool, he is already there, he just doesn't know it—so later on she is crying, Leroy is being the Big Brother, holding her—I am sad for the lady—I still think I should take her boyfriend & feed his face to a pit bull, there is just no room for him in this scenario, no more space at his trough, not w/me here—

25 September

So, this woman's name is [zzz]—a lot of trouble for nothing to gain—but she has an attractive something—also has a real asshole for a boyfriend—I have been over there twice now, end up being asked to leave by him both times—I don't go but it is still rude of him—all I want to do is his old lady, what's the deal?, the inhospitable fuckhead—oh, well, if I were him, I'd shoot me—

Fall is developing nicely, the trees haven't started to change, but you can still feel it in the air, see it in the quality of light in the afternoon—horses are growing their winter coat, bunnies are getting fat & sassy & bouncing off the walls—

30 Sept cool early am
Sat nite, tomorrow's off

So, work sucks, it's easy, pays the rent & buys me beer—but I need more money, a better job, a rich girlfriend—

THE LUNATIC BIRDS OF ILLINOIS

I

So, we are sitting here
   on our spot
      on this planet

spinning away
   from the full moon

(People on the other side
      of this planet
   sitting on their spot
spinning toward
      the full moon)

and all the while here
   the birds have been excited
like inmates in Bedlam
   an asylum of imagination
excited
   this full moon night
like lunatics locked in a Tarantula two-step
   and the birds of Illinois
      here
hours early
   spinning towards the sun
excited
   touched by this
      bright light
   of lunacy
imaginations of day light

sitting twitching on branches
   on lines
dancing Texas line dancing
   epilepsy, W. Texas style

Chuck 5.3.96

II

These thick woods—Illinois
    bowls of sound
this part of bluffs & hills
    & hollows
all rising above the Mississippi Valley
    the sound of the wind
from below & all these songs of
    lunatic birds
moon confused for daylight songs

Chuck 5.8.96

III

Lapsed Catholics & lulls
    In the conversation
water was changed into wine
    into communion
        & conversation
into urine, water to the sea
    and all this while
into the silence
    & soundless spaces
        of these lulls & lapses
the quiet of white walls
    & asylums

This raging schizoid squawking
    both harpy & harmonious
        melodious & mad
mindless purpose echoing
    endless

Vile & vicious, vulturian
    feathered reptilian
        revile these lunatic birds

ORDINARY MAN

But I'm an ordinary man

There are times when I think
    I am nobody
I'm not special

My life is that
            of fantasy
    & reality & those combinations
    of this interaction
    of myself & others

                5.16.96

            □□□

DANCING IN THE LESBIAN BAR

I went dancing in the lesbian bar—

    combination of elbows & armpits
& a slithery sweaty sweet glistening
    of anticipation—

So, the sun was in Gemini
    the moon was in Aquarius
money was in my pocket
    converse on my feet
the door, the street—

—and they were so sweet
    to each other
afterwards
    when they were alone

            Chuck 6.6.96

BEST OFFER

So, now
    that I'm older
I thought I would
    sell my soul—

The best offers
    so far—
heaven or hell,
        oblivion
            or another
                chance on the
                    wheel,
                        the rack—

So, I'm still
    holding out—
For?
    A better offer!
A man would have to be
    a fool
to sell cheap
    what he couldn't buy—
So, I might sell
    my foolishness—

                Chuck June 1996

GETTYSBURG

A human being on defense in Gettysburg—133 years
later

Jenny Wade 20 yrs old
    kneading bread
the only civilian casualty at Gettysburg

carried away by Federal soldiers
    buried in a confederate
    coffin built for a general

shoe maker—cobbler
72 yrs John Burns a civilian
fought w/150th PA volunteers

Bret Harte: "John Burns, a
practical man, shouldered his
rifle, unbent his brows & then
went back to his bees & cows"

Lt. Col. Mudge 2nd Mass. USA
    killed July '63
It's murder, but it's an order

                7.25.96

WRAPPED IN ASPHALT

So the sounds that
   are with this quiet,
       so drunk, so
  all alone
      & by yourself
          quiet dark
             time
& god is where?
  All the way where—

& the dark, dark time
   that asphalt
   that dark black asphalt
     & god & this time

& who is wrapped
  in this dark

& who is wrapped
     in this dark
   black asphalt, this god
who lays wrapped in this
    dark black asphalt
of god—

         12.96

YOUR TRUST

And this time
    your trust is not denied

& your innocent
    trust in sleep
is not denied

& somehow
    god
has time to affirm this
    & this time
your innocence
    is not to be
    denied

& god
    forgot
for a moment

that your trust
    was not to be denied

12.16.96

[NOTES ON A 1997 CALENDAR—ILLINOIS, BACK TO CHICO]

Dec 31 Don Lewis's Bday, Chris by, Luke/Canada bust

JANUARY

Marge → Cancun, Pat/Doug over, Gene called, mom • Pat is back to S.D. Pipes frozen→Vern • Marge back, Cancun, Leroy→Don's • Work dead, still frozen, sewer a mess • Vern, water, sewer open, warming up • Kathy & the brood, Kurt & Doug, Leroy & Kay run, snow & ice • Buttons→fall, Bud→ cans, work dead, storm, winter • Leroi, Kurt, Stagger Inn again, cold, windy • Gene called, Luke on phone, Indiana, Kurt, Leroy, grandma • Buttons→St. Louis, K.T. calls • Leroy & Alan, still cold, feeling better • Pat's car stolen, Dave P→ear burn • Leroy, Alan, Pat, Dave, car trip—two broken ribs, Buttons calls • Warm, Sandy at Dew Drop, Alan, Stagger w/Leroy, Vern— food, biz trip • Leroy, Alan, Stagger Inn again • A do-nothing day • A do- nothing day • Buttons ←CA, Kathy & the brood again • Buttons call 4 am, Doug, Kurt Jay, Brian, Bud's Bday—40, very cold, clearing • Dinner w/Don, Leroy, Stagger • Phone trip w/Buttons, stay home • Deli—check—Fed ex, warm, home trips, Alan over

FEBRUARY

Payday, B & C, Stagger for a burger, homeday • Early up, work slow, Alan over, kick back, Leroy over • Work, Buttons call, St. Louis w/Leroy, stoned again • Peaches, Button's call, Alan the Dickhead, rainy night • Kathy/Chris over • Gray, warm, cold • Grey, paperwork, taxes, doug by, snow—2", pkg →Buttons • Call Buttons, papers in pkg mon, Doug, Cheryl, Lauren • Worked sucked, grey snowy • Buttons call, St. Louis w/Leroy, stoned again • Left work early, depressing day, Doug, Paul over • Warmish, work hyper, Leroy→Stagger Inn & out, Stagger crowd, watch the sun come up, crash at 8 am, up at 3, back down at 7—lost day, another million brain cells gone for a dubious cause • Grey → sunny, talk w/buttons, downtown/laundry, do nothing day, happy birthday Ged • Up early clear, going cloudy, work→ paper work, work slow, Doug over, cook turkey • Cold, clear, work mostly boring, doug over & home, Leroy→stagger, toke w/Hanna, home—rain later • Stagger until midnite, strange evening, 2 hrs sleep→work→ • Library books due, Pday, rent check on Friday, bank trip

MARCH

Work→very busy, Stagger→Red's birthday • Clear, beautiful day, no Doug, bed early, no sleep tho, work—busy prep • Cool, clear, work slow, Leroy, Doug, one more day • Sick→cold, Leroy over, Doug & Lauren • Work sucks, still sick • Cold, clear, mom called, Buttons, Leroy by & bedtime, still sick • Cold flurries, bank, library, etc…Buttons' packing, kick-back day • Paper trips, house trips, Buttons 6 pm/Leroy TWA 576 • Grey, kick-back day, Leroy gone, late, lots of good-bye • Stagger for a beer • Gray, Pete Hiney, no taco • Rain, & of course work sucks • clear, cool, Stagger, Harry, Doug • Work busy, Luke? John, Alan, Doug, Dave, smoke out • Doug & Lauren, pizza, store, paper trips • Warm, cloudy, work slow, B→100.00 • Work slow, Theresa in all morn, lots of calls →Leroy→Nicci, Vern, no Doug • Stagger→Harry, Doug • Easy day, Leroy→Tempe • C & B pd, Buttons & Chuck hang out

APRIL

Sunshine, Leroy→lunch, Stagger, BS afternoon, BBQ w/Buttons • Buttons BS • St. Louis, Buttons BS • Blah, off on a Sunday, only 2 fights w/Buttons • Rain, clear, work sucks, fuck'em • Rain, bike back, B→doc, false alarm, Alan→Luke • Warm, Doug, Jay, Brian, Joel, Cheryl, Stagger, Tom Jr. fired • Nice day, pork roast Doug→Paul, Luke back Canada • Luke/Alan, Luke overnight • Laverne hired, Josh fired

MAY

Leg fracture, hitch, moving w/Doug • Moving • Mostly fucked up physically, moving, bike wreck, lost a few days • Stagger • Gray, busy • Rain, Gene called, Poophead Alan's Bday • Rain, hanging out, bills, St. Louis→Leroy, ho hum • Gray, no rain, sunny, D & C coming over early • Carol's kids, Madison, Ivory, Rowal

JUNE

Buttons→Carla • Leroy→Ft. Russell • Kick-back, stay out of trouble • Gray, sunny, strange slow day, Nicci's Bday, Stagger Inn & out • Got lucky, off at 11 am, Leroy and Matt, 4-leaf clover • Works sucks, more rain • Just another day, you bet • Doug's Bday, Ren's Bday, calls→bullshit nite • Spaced, bah

223

fucking humbug • Hot, sweat, Brandy/Staci Bday • Luke→Amber • What the fuck—Buttons flips out, Alan's a hero, I'm J. Dor • Strange days for real • Len Cohen morn, what can I say? Yesterday & today too strange—interesting, tho • There is <u>always</u> the quiet after the storm • Steady, hot, spaced, Buttons→Calif, Leroy gets shot • A/C maybe fired • Life sucks, work sucks • Rent→Vern, ha ha • Pay day, ha ha

JULY

Another day, something's bothering me • Fucking hot, sick still, Leroy over, call Gene, work really sucks • Finally cool, I feel good for the first time in a week & then the shit hit the fan—Stagger, Raymond, lost 40.00 • Spacey day, fighting w/Buttons again • Theresa is a bitch, a curse on her • Same-o same-o, just another day • Barth's, Rusty's, Leroy/Kurt over, AAA→Lauren, Alan→beer—friends? Bro! • Hot, humid, Vern→A.C., got laid • Buttons→ call/no talk, movies & nothing—fuck this place • Do nothing day, no calls, no Buttons, no nothing • D & C→cater, Alan & family, pig-out day • Town trips, compost→Alan, mellow sort of day

AUGUST

Hot, Alan→Cahokia→Luke, Belleville→Alan, the asshole once again—call →Buttons, work/BBQ→Alan • Rain, up early, Leroy all fucked up—time to leave • Raymond Bday • Luke 20 Aug Bday, 1951—1977, Leroy still fucked up • Cool, sunny, Doug Cheryl no show • Hot clear Sunday, Buttons call→ Corky • This month we start to get the fuck out of Dodge • Hillary Bday • Dave Stoeklin Bday • Vern→rent again

SEPTEMBER

Do nothing day, but done well • Rent ½→Vern • Stagger for a beer, work late, do nothing day, cancel cater job? • Appeal hearing, Edmund→bike wreck, Buttons call • Nothing new or special, packing • Ruthie's Bday, Button's moving • Linda L→Bday, Alan over, mom call visit 3-4 Oct, K.T. on phone—sick • Cool, rain, fuck'em all—deli, Nicci, stagger/Randy/Dave

OCTOBER

Cool, sunny, packing, Barth 10:30, Buttons→B.S. • Warm, sunny, interview 10:00, Leroy→gone, Vern • Barth→new job, call Buttons, mom • Hot again, work busy, Luke→sun, mom, Alan • Luke→Alan's 3 pm→Alan's→BBQ, call Linda, Buttons • Hot pm, library, Gene call→150.00 • Frost warning, travel agency, Alan, card, packing tape • Frost, sunny, packing, pizza & ice-cream pigout • Up early packing, mom's Bday • Bank, Gene, work 2-8:30, Buttons call • Work slow, phone calls, do nothing, bed early • Work dead, D&C→over & gone, packing • Town run, Doug over, lost evening, Sandy coming • UPS → packing, library, town trips, bike ride • Almost done packing, Sandy call • Cool, overcast, windy, D&C court, almost a win, hang-out & read, do nothing • Call→Luke, Cheryl, Cassen Travel, Buttons→8:30, mom, Kathy→Sandy, Barth's 2 pm—steady, easy • Grey, windy, rain, 2 mo →xmas, Luke→not home, D&C→dinner sun • Cold, rainy, time change, Barth's—8, busy → fuck, Randy → stroke • Cool, grey, do-nothing day, Cassen's→Cal, Buttons→Flt # • VE papers, fucked again, alan over, Sandy no-show, Gene • Cool, sunny, do nothing, bike ride, hanging out, Raymond, Kathy over • Alan→Don→me, call Buttons, Leroy Bday

NOVEMBER

Grey, cold, windy, leaves falling, lots of color, work slow, snow flurries • Hang out • Barth Bday • Grey, cold, packing, 100.00→Buttons • Cooking→ soup, no D&C, bed early • Up early, Buttons→call/off, Chip→hosp, library, snow pm, bed early • Post office, 8 boxes, 110.00, talked w/Buttons • Cold, grey winter sky, downtown trip, Luke→UPS 70.00, stuff moved • Finish packing, Buttons call→sick, Gene→Bday • Cold, grey, paperwork, packing • Library, store, do nothing • Cold, snow, work steady, Raymond, Alan & Kathy, Buttons→moving on, D&C→no callback, Luke→Sun • Last day at Barth's, Nancy→final check • Final cleaning, Mike→painting, goodbyes out the door, 10:30 flt • Foggy, long nite, Oakland, Buttons & the boys, Arrive Sac 3:33 AM, Sandy's Bday • Rain, drunk, up bullshitting, checking

DECEMBER

Work, lunch on the dog, laundry w/Bob & Buttons, movie, kick-back • B→ work, paperwork/sort & toss, K.T. → dinner, apply—work, Katie's • Do nothing days, starting to get that cold • Larry died • Dinner at Katie & Zoe • Rain, bah humbug, sick—do nothing day • Just another day • Grey, sunny, B.S. day • Clancy, K.T., Charles • Hang-out day • Rain, do nothing • Tree up, Bob→?? • grey, fog, phone trips, Alan→B.S. • Food bank, fuck-off • K.T.→ yard sale, payday→brewery • Work, busy day • Sunny, quit drinking • Sunny, very sick, horrible day, do nothing but whine • Sunny, Damien call, sick, shakes, turkey dinner • Better, turkey for the boys, K.T./Zoe presents • Sunny, B→work • Nice day, work slow, table busted, B→Ruthie's • Sunny, work slow, K.T.'s →moving, video/pizza, sick • Sunny, packing

THAT KIND OF MORNING

So, it's that kind of morning—
   a handful, pocketful
      of crumbled dollar bills
   & wallet full
      of ATM receipts
         no recollection
     but a scratchy maybe
        image
    more crumpled
        than the dollar bills—
brain cells & clarity
   like lint, dust particles
     & dead flaky skin things
   in with the dollar bills

OPINIONS

Good morning,
    you've reached W W Chuck
    Like they say
        down at the stockyards
    if it ain't bullshit
        we ain't got it—

Today's topic—
    opinions!

52% of all polled
    have one

37% of some of the rest
    have heard of one

part of the 11% of those
    have thought about
            one

& most of the rest
    don't give a shit—

Is that everybody?
Chuck—now—what's yours?

      10.27.97
      Edwardsville, Ill

POEM FOR LEROI: *JUST ANOTHER TACO*

Hey, Leroi—

So—you talk in drunken candor
        a can of Oly—
  kind of look at it
  slant the light
        40—45 degrees
  sit back & squint

and then tell me
  we don't have Jesus Christ
right there on the can!

      Is that a miracle
        or what?

Crown of thorns & all—
    especially the thorns & all—
of course,
    it also
        looks like a skull
a real ugly mugger with a disease—

A real lady, a Mexican lady
    does have, really,
the face of Jesus Christ
stained & sigmatatized
    on a tortilla—
down there in L.A.!

Her cousin-in-law,
    he set up an altar—
actually, a taco stand—
for the crowds
      & the worshippers, penitents
        & the skeptics—

Some in the crowds
    thought this was communion
& that the two bits & a tip,
    just a tithe—

But her cousin-in-law
    & the taco wagon
    & the understanding

$1 is more than two bits!
& anyhow,
    it still was just a taco—

Some kids—
    down there in Brazil—
    slums & barrios
    garbage dumps & shacks
    accordioned in ravines—

So, they found
    some radioactive waste
& they just played with it—

& they said it sparkled,
sparkled in the sun!

You hold it 40-45 degrees & just squint
why, you could just see
    the face of Jesus Christ
smiling through a rainbow
    & the sparkle of the sky

Of course,
    it also grinned
        the smile of a skull—

Of course,
    a real pretty lover
        with a disease—

I had this friend once
   his name was David
& once in a while
   we would get drunk on beer
we drank a lot of beer
   that Oly & the thorns
   ranted & raved & ridiculed
       injustices, darkness in the night

& then I heard
   he died of aids,
just another kid in Brazil—

"Fuck the fucking fuckers"
he thought that sort of said it all
   giving some credit
      to my ignorance
      & my drunken verbosity

and then, I heard he died

& I wondered,
   when he looked up
      into the face of his lover,

what he saw
in that 40-45 degree light
through squint & sweat—

the face of his lover?
   the thorns?

A really pretty lover
   tho with a disease,
or just another taco—

& Jesus Christ
   smiled through the rainbow
sparkled through sky,
   & off of grinning skull,

that diseased smile of a mugger

while,
    down there, down there
the boxes
    were lowered into the dirt
& the mist that morning
    sparkled in the sun—

& if you just would squint
    40-45 degrees
Jesus Christ would just smile
that grin, just another taco—

Chuck 6.27.97

RELEASED FROM MY PROMISE

In 1995 Chuck and Buttons moved to Illinois, Carver's Canned Condos (Vernon's trailer park). Buttons hated Illinois, we have snow, a thing she dreaded. Once traveling with them cross country Buttons lost control on "black ice" in Montana. I was sleeping in the back seat and awoke off the interstate in a ditch. She gave me the keys (Chuck didn't drive) and said "Drive." We stopped and picked up a fifth of vodka and a quart of orange juice and that held her together through Snoqualmie pass in Washington (chains required but she had none, but I am used to snow). Anyway, Buttons headed back to California after falling on the sidewalk in the snow. Chuck stayed and said that this was the end of their marriage. He drank more and got taken home by a lady named Liza and thought he had found romance, but Liza told him he snored and not to call her again. He was shattered. I introduced him to another local lady who I know had a thing for Capricorns (Chuck was born on Christmas day). Again he launched into another romantic scenario. Meanwhile Buttons called me and asked me to stay with Chuck and I said I would. I moved in and things were OK until he decided that he wanted to go to California and was drinking more heavily. One day I came to the Canned Condo to find all my things in the driveway. I breathed a sigh of relief at being released from my promise. We remained friends and at the end of 1997 he flew back to Buttons and California.

Leroi

We had great times together and talked of everything under the sun and in space. There was the day was when he was barred from "The Stagger Inn", escorted out the door by Gary Meyer in a headlock. I wrote a poem during this time:

CBL THE 3RD

Mayhem, motion, madness and more
  Walked off the job and drifted into
      a headlocked exit from his favorite
          saloon-an unforgivable sin in his world.

Lost the compass heading, fire in the hold
  Sargasso sea-albatross around his neck,
      cold slow wind and hot quick language,
          the state of the ship and ship of states.

Prairie schooners don't sink like ocean vessels
  airplanes require air and the ticket to ride
      and yet he hears the sirens song from the west
          2,000 miles, a desert and mountains away

Bitten and driven mad by the siren and gypsy moth
  run aground in the flatland, sea of corn and prairie
grass
      holding the wheel, telescope and sextant tightly
          waiting for the moon to cause the tide to rise

                                        Leroi

PRIDE

An Article Of Faith!

    What do I have?
I have pride!
   Like the black man
       of South Africa,
I have pride!
   The fierce blast
       of the summer's heat
tearing away
       even the memory
   of that child-like spring,
when,
    like an awakening
       from slumber, a hibernation,
with a fierce remembering &
   a roar of challenge,
again, that hunger for renewal,
   that almost desperate need
to grasp the radiation of
   the blazing, blazing sun—
& the day smells of flint,
    waves of heat over
       dancing lizards,
silent wisps of cobweb,
    drifting hot touches
       on the sides of thorn bushes—

Pride
   like moisture
giving back a life,
   a flowering,
       promises
of fertilization
      & continuation,
a fierceness for life—

Pride
    like a mother's tears
washing over a child's death,
    a grieving over
the high payment
        of life, of
God,
    such a shylock,
this fierce indebtedness of life—

Pride
    like a tearing wound
a bloody rage, screaming conflict
    a dark seepage
spreading thru white hot spikes
    of sand—

Death,
    such a price to ask
for these visions of freedom—

ON RAILS

Two weeks ago,
I came upon a butterfly
lying broken & twisted,
waiting beside a fallen leaf—

Today it is winter,
   cold & grey,
dark clouds race across the sky
   like the great dark flocks
of birds that are blown
   along by the winds
coming down from Canada—

the sun sets dead center
   in the V of the R.R. tracks
way off in the distance; from there,
   like some great solar locomotive
on rails, it travels ever westward
   until, reaching the sea
it slips under that watery horizon

SEASONS

Thoughtless watching,
    aimless walking
through this Illinois countryside—

These autumn woods
    waiting, silent fields
dark & musty smelling,
    take within themselves
the seeds of imagination
    to release them later—

Seeds pushing green shoots
    upwards towards the sun,
breaking open the earth
    & reaching, stretching up,
Oh, Lord,
    just to grab some warmth—

The country here awaits
    just one heavy frost,
        and then,
claim the old ladies
    on the early morning bus,
always experts on such matters
    as the weather,
and then, summer
    & even this late fall
will be gone, and
    winter gradually
& seemingly forever
    will take back the land—

COUNTRY SATURDAY

The trees here are turning
    greens to yellows & orange,
down the autumnal spectrum
    to red, then finally
to brown & dying,
    lying in gutters
or piled in small mounds
    at the base of trees,
waiting for a country Saturday,
    the smells of burning October—

           □□□

CHANGING

So, the year is changing again,
    the heat of summer cools,
all those bursts of green growth
    have slowed and are falling
        back—

gravity, glimpses
    of grey winter—

But the leaves of Autumn again,
    the harvest moon ripe above,
all the colors of sunlit days
    are glowing silver
coldness, blueprint
    of white winter—

UNEXPECTED

Summer is gone,
    not slowly faded
but swiftly,
    overnight
and now it is Autumn,
    chilling winds
high overhead, faint white
    clouds from Canada—
taste the chill off
    those mighty land-locked seas
far north of these
    flat river plains—

In the woods lining our road
    the squirrels are jumping
high among thinning foliage,
    sending down small flutters of leaves
as they search frantically
    to fill they stores
that are not quite ready, unexpected
    as the early winter closes—

MEMORIES

An old man on a bench,
cold grey October day,
sits going thru his
memories,
a book, well worn,
paged thru slowly,
sometimes falling open to
well read pages,
other times
passages read after
a lifetime
and new meanings emerge—

Across the path, covered
by the leaves of Autumn,
a cloak protecting the earth
through the dying time of winter,
a small boy cracks the binding
of a new book & stares—

Elk Grove Ca
29 May 98 Cancer Moon
Weather is strange

Rolling Stones – I'm so hot for her
& she's so cold

Gemini Sun Vibes – the twins are twisted these days – El Nino is more than a strange bedfellow – Mother Nature gone a bit neurotic or maybe just tired of her favorite son, Mr. Man, His Self – an amalgam of conceit & charm & testicles – She, Mom Natural, just a bit ready for PMS & sorta tired of him, no longer wanting to filter his whining and Yama Yama Mama BS monologueing, has basically decided to just ex him, spit in the soup & bone, bone appetite – Darwin would sharpen pencils in his grave, this a chance to append a footnote, Mother Nature having a bad hair day.

16 June 1998
Elk Grove CA

Just another day
W/Charlie Bernie & Mary Bob
She just got a little meaner
He just quit another Job

16 June 98

Psychic haiku
Chainsaws
Chunks on the
Ceiling
Rave, rave
The howlings
Of Ginsburg
So much babble

18 July Hotter than hell
Moon – Gemini
El Nino & La Nina

New music CD 'Caliente' w/Willie & the wolf – flamenco & violin
And keyboard w/Rick Brown –Django style
Old music CD Miles in 'Spain/Sketches – Flamenco & the blues/Larr
w/Gil Evans
Ernie Royal w/Miles/Willie Royal w/Willie & the Wolf…?
Melancholia, sadness, Tristessa
Miles & Evans
 Eruption & composition
Chaos & order
Jazz Fractals
The mind rages for understanding

29 Aug 98 summer still
Scorpio/Sag moon

Miles Davis—Kinda Blue w/kind of an upbeat—summer still
hanging on, 105 degrees is not a sign of early fall—Virgo sun,
hysterical discipline, wannabe Capricorn—Scorpio is the only
Autumn sign, the only sign that points to the end, to the beginning—a
break between extremes—Libra is too mellow, too easy, that
harmonies balance is just another straddling of the fence—Sag is
shaking hands w/Janus, opening the way for winter—

1998 CALENDAR NOTES

MARCH

Call: Mel's/Brewery, day-off • Fighting w/Buttons, Casa Gomez dinner •
Call: D & C, Lauren, Bob, recycle, Linda • Katie, check/phone bill, payday •
Rain, gray, cool, Buttons ends Thursday as she began—a poophead • Grey,
wet, slow day, Bob→BS & beer • Grey, warm, rain, Jeff sick, work w/Angie,
B & C do a movie & a meal • Nice day, thunderstorms, Galt flea market,

drive around, do nothing, nice day • Plumbing, K.T over for supper, yard work, etc • Cold, clearing, work slow, B→Ruth, C→bed early • Raining

APRIL

Cool, warm cloudy, kick-back afternoon • Bob pd table, out to county, went downhill next, bed, bye • Project day, pig-out & stoned, Katie over, Gene phone • do nothing days • Buttons, K.T., Zoe off to Woodland • Up early, buttons back early • Mixed weather, work dead, K.T. over, laundry • Clear, warm, do nothing house trips, B→Ruthie's • Work for buttons • lawn work, Bob→Sac • Sunny, work slow, busy, Clancy Bday • Work busy, biker party, K.T., Zoe Bday party, Damien/Lori, Clancy • Payday, Ruthie→home, B & C →Chico, 45 & the river, Erica & Wolf, Chapmantown, overnite→Clancy • Up early, cool, clear, Cohasset→Elk Grove→Bob's/bank/broke, Gene→ 150.00→load stuff from storage—K.T.→supper • Paid rent, B of A/library, K.T. over, bed early, no sleep • Up early, grey—rain, Zoe • Up early, clear, weed-eating • Up early, yardwork, broke lawnmower w/pipe, fuck-off rest of day • Warm→hot, do nothing • Work, nothing new • Gene→fri/sat am

MAY

Fixed lawnmower • 484.00 bank • Net 347.00 + 6.5 tips • Grey, cool, Gene →visit, supper w/K.T., beer blitz • Very cool, Gene→Kt, western days supper • Rain/sun, work so/so, Buttons→Ruthie's, movies/bed ho hum • Paper work, money things • Money day, lawn-mower fucked, Tris→e-mail • Paperwork, bills, store, library • Sunny→grey, read all day • sunny, grey, K.T. over w/Zoe • Buttons to Ruthie's, me & the dog the rest of the day • Rain again, home again, Buttons lose 100.00, Jeff call→potatoes • K.T. over for supper, Buttons→job interview→owner • Buttons→2 week notice • Warm, Buttons→Corky, Buttons screwed • Chico w/Corky, kick-back day • Warm, windy, back went out, fucked up day • Back still out, Leroy/Don called, payday • Sunny, back still out • sunny, warm, back still fucked, home again • Work slow, B→up & down • Grey, cool, fuck-around day—K.T./B vibes, dinosaurs Zoe • Up early, cool, grey, called into work, Bob's/dinner &

JUNE

Spaced out day, Alan call, Hillary • Hang out day, do nothing, spag cooking
• Sunny→grey, movie, bed at 8 pm • Read, shower, work • Steady, busy,
long day, B K.T.→dine home alone, ok, payday • K.T. & Zoe store, Buttons
bedtime • Work steady, leg of lamb, do nothing • Inside/outside day, yard
work, plant room • Back hurts, bank, movie & nothing evening • Grey, cool,
back is fine, new schedule for July, ho hum • Hot, sun, early work, 7 am,
busy, steady, Vern → 87.50, Buttons → dinner • Work—B.S., Buttons →
Bob's/Bob, bullshit • Slow, steady, Buttons→bar, Bob, drinking w/the boss,
Mel vibes, Pete • Wasted, warm, lost day, Buttons & K.T. dinner, up late,
lost day, lost nite • Warm→hot, still out there, just stay home • Hot, slightly
hung over, work busy, steady, B→Ruthie's • Busy, late, hot, C & B & T.V. •
Movie & a beer, gone to bed • Up early, back bothering me, work dead •
K.T.→BBQ w/B & baby Z • Rent/PG&E pd, ins pd, lunch & dinner out,
another one just like the other one • Do nothing day, pizza & a video • Work
steady, smooth, dinner from Casa Gomez • Warm, windy, work slow, Tris &
Eric→CA trip • Bob's→B & Jeff, smoke, video, all my money • Spacey, do
anything day • Yardwork, goof-off, movies & dinner

JULY

Slow work, ended fucked, reading, etc...B→Ruthie's, Talk→Tris • Home &
a movie, dinner Gomez • Hot, work, sucker, B→Ruthie sick, Tris in late,
bed early • Over to Bob's, K.T. & Zoe, Tris & Howard, 55→smoke • Off
afternoon, to the zoo→home→here→Casa Gomez, payday • Dumb movie,
afternoon, lazy evening • Hot again, flea mkt/Galt? dinner w/KT & T & E &
B, every one says see you later • B→Ruthie's, Angie→vacation • KT over,
Buttons & her soap opera • Corky med/foot, movie day • Hot, breezy, bike
ride, KT's for dinner, Zoe, fun • Lazy afternoon, wash machine out • Call-
out Italian & do nothing—Tris back? • Slow, mellow, 100+ degrees, movie •
Hotter, fast start work, busy finish, B→Ruthie's • 110 degrees+, shopping,

AUGUST

Warming up—100 degree—work open early, busy all day, dinner & bed •
Bob's club, B&J no show, dinner→Casa Gomez, hot—hot—105 degrees •
108 degrees, home & do nothing • Up early, open 5 am, work alone, steady,
busy, very hot, 111 degrees, off work, weird trip • Jeff in & out, Bob,
Buttons, beer, tv/kick-back, 50.00 → Buttons, perm • Steady, warm, B →
Ruthie's • Cool, up 2 am, fuckaround, Buttons→car door, Ruthie died fri
nite • Strange day, D & G & C & us, phone all day, Corky→MH & out • Up
moving Ruthie's drugs, alcohol & bullshit, arguing, on the wagon & off to
bed • Home alone, in bed, Bob Geo→truck, back to bed, 1 day sober • Up,
better, weak, Clean-it-up time, shop Cork, services, people coming down •
Life still sucks but it goes on, Ruthie out of apartment • Bank—home—
cleaning—phone calls, Squeak→Wyo, 4 dys • Services→11 am, G & L + C
& S, low-key/over, back here/noise, then gone—quiet—quiet, off wagon •
KT & Zoe over for brkfst, veg type of day, supper & veg, some more &
more • Yardwork, job vibes—resume→KT, calls/apps, slow, quiet evening •
Erica→call back Annie Meyers, B & K→Ruthie's ashes • Drinking, fucking
up • Fuck this, been here before • Drinking at Bob's • Hungover, still
drinking, making an ass out of myself • Sun, on the wagon again, depressed
• Job search again, feel better • Car running, needs tune-up, laundry—job
search • Fuck this Sears sort of strife, woose—fuck'em • Hot still, Hillary's
Bday, B & K & Zoe→Monterey, bullshit, fuck'em • Bullshit

SEPTEMBER

August really sucked, this was the pivot point—no more, life goes on→job
→B.S., etc • Hot, fuck Elk Grove • Hot, fuck Denny's • Hot • KT Bday •
Beautiful day, new job • Hot, Buttons→assanine • Hot, stupid • Buttons→
Bob's kids day, quit drinking again • Corky→rehab, Corky→back...& forth
& back • do nothing day, Sunrise→hire • Weather perfect, work too easy,
Fri nite→fuck it • Physical 130/80, beer/smoking, B→sick • Ceasare goes
home—work solo—hangout • Work solo, hangout & drink beer • Cork back
→detox bound • Sick • Off

OCTOBER

Corky→rehab & back again, bullshit as usual • Work, B.S. at home • Alice sucks, so?! • Easy day, busy, easy, recycle • Noise, confusion, full moon coming • Up too early, work w/Barb, negotiate w/Bob • Bills→rent, phone,

pg&e, fuck off day, drinking • Beautiful weather, blew most of my money, cooking, ride in park, call Linda, Paul, Cheryl, Luke, Lauren • Corky back, B→bus sta. • KT & Zoe by • Turkey soup, work goes easy, fucking w/Corky • Kick back afternoon, Corky walks 13 mi • Day off, do nothing, Buttons tries to off the dog, same old bullshit • Work at 10 am, confused, hectic, cold treatment, B→hiding money—SSI? • Nice day, supper w/Buttons, Corky in Sac • Working the clock—B→supper, wining & dining, Corky→V.A. • Busy, mellow, perfect weather, Corky→home, B & BS→blah blah • Corky

NOVEMBER

Drug test, do nothing days • Full moon→Gemini, waiting on Walmart, Corky→job-hunting • Grey stay home day—do nothing, movie w/B, bed at 4, up at 10→graveyard • Gene's Bday • B & K & Zoe→zoo • Jazz club→4 CD • Kick-back waiting days→• B→KT & Zoe shopping, Cork→sleeping in, do nothing day, rain coming, Buttons/B.S. SS checks again—fuck'em • Hanging out, tired, getting sick, Buttons /BS still • Run around day, paid early, bed, no sleep, work graveyard, sick, no sleep • Meat loaf, save a turkey, work sucks, still sick • Raining, cold, Buttons→KT, once more home

DECEMBER

Corky→gone→rip off, etc…calls→police, Kelly, Church, hosp, etc…• Winter weather, hang out with the dog • rain, grey→do nothing day, go to work, be a jerk • Home all day, do nothing, missed supper, too tired, call—Clancy, house→demolition • Tris→package/call, KT dinner • Weather miserable, call in sick, Corky→Chico, fuck him • Cool→sunny, xmas trips, house/paperwork • Work, bikes, stuff, bah humbug • Vito, my man • Payday, bank/Bob, hang out, xmas • Present wrapping, KT & Zoe, xmas eve • Turkey day at KTs • Hang out at KTs • Do nothing, KT's mobile

Katie & Zoe, Time & Place Unknown

I carry his love for me in my heart and no matter what "other" people think and/or feel, I was his daughter and as much as I know he was an asshole, I did still love him, a lot, and he "knew" he was an asshole, he even apologized to me for being such a stupid, self centered asshole. He actually respected me for telling him like it was and no matter what anyone thinks, with the exception of Buttons and Zoe, he loved me more than anyone in the world, I know that in my heart.

Katie

The Id, the ego &
The super ego—
The father, the son & the holy ghost—
   If your ego can't handle
      being called an asshole
      once in a while,
  just get rid of it,
      it's just another luxury
      that you can't afford—

Chuck 9.14.98

247

RIP-OFF

These men are pirates
    not IBO IBO
        landlocked traditions

men that rule over most
    of the earth

these men make you
    into paper dolls
your life is compressed
    distilled onto
a disk, a floppy disk

why rip-off a bank
    when
you can rip-off mankind?

                    July 13.00

                □□□

AFRICAN PYGMY MUSIC

Bees dancing
    buzzing & humming in a hive
circles & buzzing & humming
    hot dusty sun bright Africa
        stomping lives
men & women
    stomp stomp
rolling onomatopoeia
        off their tongues
throwing other sounds out
    joy & monotony loved
        celebrated
this a word picture of African pigmy music—

SKETCHES

Niagara Falls, man & his mind
    the ego of desperation
less than the sweat, the sheen
    on the balls of god
every molecule an everest
    mountains are a joke
        of size-ness—

                □□□

A bench, a book
    a beer
embarkation
    on a bus
on a bus route
    w/bus stops—

                □□□

Bus stop
    nature walk
on the way to work
    star thistles
        & dead kittens
magpies, crows
    constant conflict
baby quails crossing the road
    momma qail, overhead
hovering, haunted cries
babies gone, dead
    magpies & crows
fighting, screaming challenges
        "What! What! What! What!"—

                7.27.00

DAYS

Friday, a day
   like Saturday, another day
      a day
pearls on a string
   sparkle, jewels on a string
(a trout line on a murky river, dead
     catfish & bleach bottles)
   everyday is yesterday
tomorrow is a jewel
   pearl on a string
the future is anticipation
   god grins
the sweet glory
   of the blood
plunder of treasure
   the rape
the death of today
   the glory of meaningless
         Tomorrows—

        Chuck 7.27.00

S.P.C.A

I might be dumb
   enough
to talk to dogs
   but I'm still
smarter than the dog!

Ask the dog—

        12.29.00

THE FACE OF JESUS

Once there was a taco

& on it
    the face of jesus
& the shrine was greasy
    & on two wheels
& they made a small fortune
    a small Mexican fortune

god on the face of a taco
    marketing this
they lined up
    they ate
    & prayed
    & cried
business brisk
    god is a great draw
            a smiling fool
almost a used car salesman
    or a smiling lawyer
    cheesy-face total-page
    photo on the back cover
    of a phone book

7.27.00

Clancy & Chuck, Chico, Around 2000

I first met Chuck about 35 years ago in Japan. Although we were nodding acquaintances, I really didn't get to know him until we were both transferred to a new flight squadron in Okinawa. There we hung out with the same people, listened to similar music and discovered we liked a lot of the same books. One time we discovered that we had both independently come to the conclusion that we never wanted to be the center of the universe. Not a big thing but we both thought it profound. (I forget what we had been drinking.)Running into Chuck was the furthest thing from my mind when I returned to Monterey after the unpleasantness of the Far East, but he was one of the first people I ran into on the street. In fact, I ended up living in his garage for a while. This began about thirty years of living together or in each others houses, hitchhiking around the country and in general living rich and full, out of the mainstream lives.I've tried to think about what defined Chuck and I gave up. The man was complex. He could be a saint and he could just as easily be a complete asshole. Or he could be both at the same time. And he could change in a nanosecond. One night, in a house we lived in together, he went to bed with long hair and a full beard. At three in the morning he got up, cut off the hair, shaved off the beard and got back into bed. I awoke that morning to Buttons Screaming. The next step, of course, is that Buttons tried to kill him; and she almost got away with it

because he was laughing so hard he could barely stand up. Change wasn't just an acquaintance; it was an intimate companion.

But while you couldn't define Chuck (at least with any psychology I've ever heard of) there were a couple of things that were pretty constant about him. One, he laughed. A lot. Two, and most importantly, he always remained himself, whether you were a five-year-old child or the President of the United States. You would get pure unadulterated essence of Chuck. This, of course, made small children adore him and pissed off most every authority figure he ever met. It made his job history a thing of legend. As my 80 year old mother commented after the last time she met him, "He does use the 'F' word constantly, but he's very charming."

Now that he's gone I miss him something awful, and I think about him a lot and I take comfort in that because, when I reminisce about the events in my life that were exciting, meaningful and hysterically funny, Chuck was, and is, there. If he went to heaven, as he should, he's probably already pissed off God; if he went to hell, as he should, well, he's probably pissed off Satan too (I did mention he has a problem with authority figures, didn't I?). I'm giving odds that he has a time-share condo in both places.

Clancy Gherke, Friend
Chico, CA, September 2008

Buttons, Time & Place Unknown

April showers, May flowers
FOR MY WIFE

"Just a dirty, stinky old man, no job, look at you." This from the little woman, albatross and bone heavy upon me. She knows how many jobs I've had, it never lasted, she is surprised that I don't care. Get a job, quit a job. Bob Dylan's birthday came & went, Jerry Garcia is still dead—

CBL 4.25.01

254

A FEW JOBS OVER THE YEARS
FROM A NOTEBOOK, 2004

60—64 Assumption HS cafeteria • June 63—Sept 64 Dog & Suds, Cahokia, Ill • Oct 63—Jan 64 Mcdonalds • Sep 64—Sep 68 USAF • Oct—Dec 68 Reed Rubber, Sauget Ill • Oct—Dec 68 Famous Barr, St. Louis, MO • Jan—Mar 69 Famous Barr again • Apr—June 60, Bata Shoe, Md • July—Sep 69, Bata Shoe again • Oct 69—Mar 70, John Tenant Homes, Pacific Grove, CA • Apr 71—Dec 72, Beacon Gas, Pacific Grove, CA • Oct 73—Mar 74, Szabo Food, Monterey Peninsula College, Pacific Grove • 1974, Ceramics Dept., Monterey Peninsula College • Restaurant Property Development, Oct—Dec 73 • Dec 73, ½ day, Salvation Army • Jan 74—Mar 75, Ace Pizza • Oct 75, Candle Light Restaurant, Collinsville, Ill • Apr—June 76, Ventana, Big Sur, CA • Sep 76—Oct 76, Sicilian Restaurant, Chico, CA • Apr 77, Western Growers, Chico, CA • June 78—Aug 78, USDA, Arizona • Jan 78—June 78, Ruby's El Ranchito, Chico, CA • Jan—June 79 & Oct 79—Mar 80 & Sept—Dec 80 at Ruby's, Chico, CA • July 79 5th & Ivy Restaurant, Chico • June 79—Mar 80 Ken Mar, Chico • Oct 82 & Jan—June 83 Ruby's again • Jun—Nov 83 BJ's Restaurant • Jan 84 Smuckers • June 84 CCDCC • an 87—Mar 88 CCDCC • Jan 88 CCDCC again • Oct 84—Apri 86 Chico Cheese • June—July 84 Feather River Pottery • 87 Discovery World, Chico • May 86—87 WTC, Chico • June 88 Mello Morsels, Chico • Nov 88—May 89 Sucia Reef, Washington State • Jan—Mar 88, Karen's, WA • Mar—June 88 Oy Vey, WA • 89 Best Little Restaurant, WA • 89 Cobbler House, WA • 89—90 HMIT, WA • 89 19th Hole, WA • Nov 90—May 92, Secret Harbor, WA • 93 Village Café, Chico • 93 Golden Waffle, Chico • 93—2001 Cory's, Chico • 93—94 Oakmont, Chico • 94—95 Twin Oaks, Chico • 95 Downtown Deli, Edwardsville, Ill • 95, 96, 97, Do Drop Inn, Edwardsville, Ill • 95, Downtown Deli, Edwardsville, Ill • 97, Barth's, Edwardsville, Ill • 97, Downtown Deli, Edwardsville, Ill • Dec 97—Jan 98, Elk Grove Brewery, Sacramento, CA • 98 Mel's Dogs, Sac, CA • 98 (1 day) El Dorado Foods, Sac, CA • 98—99 Wal Mart, Sac • 98 Career Staff, Sac • 99 Bob's Club, Sac • 99-2000 Twin Oaks, Sac • 2000—2001 Nella Oil, Sac • 2001 Twin Oaks, Chico, CA • 2001 Bar X, Chico • 2002 Roses & Ivy, Chico • 2002 Sperion, Chico • 2003, Kellerman, Chico • 2003 Speedy Burrito, Chico • 2004, IHSS, Chico

83 jobs, 1963—2004

HOUSE OF GLASS

Economy of America—
a house of glass
built on sand,
on a bedrock of
    illusion,
architecture of
    dreams,
        blueprints of
                delusions—

                02.06.01

May 18 01

got the old
"pissed off ol' lady
& looking for a job" blues

27 Nov 01

Well, Buttons back, not quite the same-o same-o but seems like a bit more
give than take—Need a day off, w/sun & no hassles—some new clothes, a
car, money in the bank, something to do, tired of waiting, working so I can
go to work—Bored, fucking bored

Spring
        this lull
winter storms
        waiting—
the crocus again

Corkus Christianus
        a study in
banal retentive
        religious ruminations
Pompous Pilate
Judas Escargot
        on a half shell

12.6.01

E-mail from Pat; friendly fire

12.19.01

Kmart shopping spree, new clothes, x-mas presents, bus riding, strange as
any other anywhere—WTC, old ladies, homeless, disabled, strange people
wearing tin foil turbans, funny clothes, people w/metal things in their faces,
pastel hair, skinheads & tattooed ladies, bored belligerent bus drivers & of
course us, Chuck & Buttons, normal

With Luke & Alan @ Luke's 50th Birthday, Centerville, Il, August 20, 2001

In Chuck's later years, after he returned to California, I talked with and saw him less often. I suppose that if I was older or Chuck younger, we would have done more things together. I'll always remember Chuck. He had a good heart. A good mind. I'll always love him in my own way.

Luke

drunk/dreamer/poet/artist/shaman

we showed each other the door

Alan Luetkemeyer, Brother
Edwardsville, Il, June 25, 2008.

258

AN ASS WHIPPING IN ELK GROVE

It was maybe 2002. Chuck and Buttons lived in an apartment in Elk Grove, CA, outside of Sacramento, over a biker joint where Chuck tended bar. The owner was a big and burley and surly biker ex-convict who was bigger and stronger and younger and meaner than chuck and to whom Chuck gave a begrudging respect, who he saw perhaps as a measure of himself. They didn't always get along; they'd exchanged words on occasion. It was an alpha dog situation. I think Chuck may have deliberately antagonized the guy to challenge himself. One day Chuck called me. He was upset. He said he had confronted his boss in the parking lot and insulted him. The big man shined him on so Chuck punched him in the face. The guy shook it off and hit him back hard, knocking him onto the pavement, then proceeded to kick him in the ribs, the head, the groin, whatever Chuck couldn't cover up fast enough. Finally the guy quit and walked away saying, I should have fucking killed your dumb ass! Chuck was left groaning on the ground with his pain and humiliation.. When he related this incident to me on the phone, his voice quavered. He was ashamed, on the verge of crying. He asked me how he ought to deal with this humiliating defeat. I said, "Hey, you got your ass kicked by a younger, stronger, bigger and badder dude than yourself that you stupidly picked a fight with to prove some meaningless point, so what did you expect? Let it go, he kicked your ass, it's nothing to be ashamed of, forget about it." I think he appreciated the advice. Afterwards he was less humiliated...but a little more humble: the self-image of being a mean mother fucker had been put into perspective.

Gene

Sat 11.02

Going back to work w/LOL
Mother's day
Sunday brunch—out the door
at 8:10/back 1:30-2, back again
mon am—the grind
is still there, and I'm back
on the block-

Sun 12.02

Mother's day brunch—easy
day—omelets, fruit salad, etc…

Mon 13.02
Tri tip, mashed potatoes
easy day—making money
Buttons home—tension

Tues 14.02

Salmon Casserole—it sucked
Busy Buttons—still tension

June 1.02

Up early, cooler, quiet
day off from the J.O.B.

Work is mellow, need to move
forward, develop style w/menu
ordering—need new ideas, more feedback—
develop a dessert/diabetic menu—
need more time at work,
money needs to be stashed
taco stand by '03/part time
work till '04, then retire
from the job—

6.29.02

Goofing in Cohasset
Joy Of Cooking CD'ing
recipe reading
Boy from Illinois

10.22.02
Autumn in Illinois
October Fest & apples

So, one more time, can't go home again,
but I got here – the land of Miles Davis
& farmers – apples & the turning of the leaves
sitting in the sun, horse farm—acreage
bird dog puppies & field corn, cat fish ponds
& soybeans—brick laying & apple plucking
quiet times & bullshit chucking—god told
me to mind my own business, so I am—
cut the cards & deal, win, lose or draw
how much more can a man ask—

10.24.02
cold, very moody

Another day down—tired, chainsaw
tired—cut & bucked ½ of a giant oak
lots of fun, but physically tired—feels
good actually, but gravity is being an
asshole lately—chain saws, beer and
tremendous urination, a man's wet dream

Wood stove, candles & kerosene lamps
30 chickens, 7 cats, 4 dogs, 3 horses
& ½ million lunatic birds, hysterical
chatter chirping birds, in the
orchards in the woods – coyotes
foxes, raccoons & possum, red necks
& negroes, little old ladies & bingo

1 July 03
Chico summer

So, another cross country trip—Stl to Sac
6 months in Il, winter, grey cold snow—
lots of wasted time—almost stress free,
no job, lots of cancelled work—Alan &
the law, fuck his attitude; D & C on the farm,
lots of wasted time & energy—Luke, worth the visit, a
nice Luetkemeyer, who would have thought?!

RAPED

    Raped by time
no consent
    just the brutal taking
the slow seduction
    almost accepting
the hands
    that would not stop
the forcing

        Sep.21.03

□□□

CELEBRATION?

How long ago,
    the traditions of man,
    man transcribing the rituals
    god patterns whispering
    of a vague understanding
    of wrinkle on a walrus
Striations/strata define celebration

        Oct.13.03 Sean's B.day

LUNATIC NOISE

This fascination with car crashes
   guns
       death by killing
          the noise
             the lunatic noise
                push past the numbness
                sensation filters

                Feb.1.04

   □□□

NOISE

filled with rage
   burning babies at Waco
     a dead mother
       Ruby Ridge
a fuck-you farewell to the feds

kids in trash cans
   kids in the cooler
of a 7-11 lay down & die
   a Two dollar rip-n video
10 seconds of fame
   25 to life in re-runs

rage – outrage
   noise...noise

CRAZY CREEPS

I'm sorry, beg your pardon,
    what, this?
Me eating
    an umbrella,
this shocks you?

    Crazy creeps
        on tiny cat claws—

                        Chuck 4.5.02

    ☐☐☐

CRAZY

One of the only things
    you count on
with a crazy person
    is that they are always
to do what you don't expect

Otherwise,
    what's the sense
        of being crazy—

                Chuck

HUMAN MAN

I'm becoming an old man
 a human man
 a too very human man
my life is in limestone
 shelf upon shelf
becoming that fossil,
 that imprint
 that will puzzle
 so many
 in the far
 future—

3.10.94

DYING FIRST

It was 2003 or 2004. Buttons was still alive. She and Chuck were living in Elk Grove, CA, in a large rambling house on a large untended lot on the side of the road destined to be razed and the lot sold, hence he got cheap rent. He worked the cash register at a gas station/convenience store down the road. I'd spent the night, we'd drank beer and bullshitted till the night was over, then I crashed on a mattress on the floor. The next morning, 5 am, Chuck's up having a beer and a joint. I join him for old time's sake, he has a few more beers, then I drive him to his job. Inside, he takes over cash register duties from the Mexican night shift girl who gives him a friendly Buenos Dias. *He logs onto the cash register and counts the money, does the little take-over routine of his duties, and I say I'm going to go now, drive back home, and he walks me outside. He's pretty wasted at 6 am at the start of his shift and he says, as I open my car door and turn around to say* Later, Bro, *he gives me this serious deep and loving look and he says,* Just don't die before me, ok? *It's 6 am and he's wasted and a little bent over and his palsied hand is doing its best dying fish imitation and he's no fool about what's left ahead in his life, not much, and he says,* Just don't die before me, ok? *And I say* Ok, *and I didn't.*

Gene

266

Chuck & Buttons, Last Year Together, Chico, 2004

BABBLING BACK

Old as a brook
    bab
        bab
           babbling
her way
    back to God

           Chuck, 4.24.94

FRAMED IN THE REAR VIEW MIRROR

Chico, CA, 1994. The memorial for Buttons was in Chapman Town, at Chuck's friend Erica's house. Family and friends gathered inside and outside in the yard and milled about on the porch. There was some talk of Buttons, not much. There was small talk, drunk talk. It was a beer fest. Chuck was wasted, which now seemed to be a permanent condition. He was still large, not shriveled away yet, but he was bent, as much from the weight of life lately as from bad health. He had a beer in one hand and the other flopped around at his side, a condition of his failing liver. He didn't say much to anyone, he wasn't spoken to much, he stood off to the side most of the time. He looked around vacantly; people walked around him; it was like he wasn't there, like he was a ghost at his dead wife's funeral, like he resided more in her time and space than he did in the boisterous world of the living around him. I left early; it was a depressing scene and I had a long drive home. Chuck walked me out to the road. We embraced, I said something, he said something, I don't remember what. As I drove away I looked in my rear-view mirror. Chuck stood at the side of the road, alone and bent, watching me go. He raised an arm slowly and waived. I waived back. I cried as I drove away and he got smaller and smaller, framed in the rear-view mirror, disappearing from my sight and my life. I watched him watching me go till I turned the corner and he was gone.

Gene

I feel like a walkabout in someone else's dream

Chuck 5.5.03

The Final Days

2005—2006

Photographs
Betty Remembers: *From The Other Side*
Gene Remembers: *Four For The Road; Going To Sleep*
Zach Remembers: *A Man At Peace*
Alex Remembers: *Lost, Unhappy, Bitter & Irredeemable*
Damien Remembers: *Tough As Nails*
Sandy Remembers: *I Miss Everybody*
Katie Remembers: *Fine By Each Other*
Michele Remembers: *Farewell Kiss*

POEMS

Who Will Eat & Who Will Serve
Winter Of My Death
Fighting Death

Death Certificate

WHO WILL EAT
& WHO WILL SERVE

(For Leonard Cohen)

Down a hall as long as a lifeline,
old men sit at a few tables,
younger men sit quietly
on straight-backed chairs.
Quieter still, boys serve the old men.
Tonight they carry out a dead man.
A young man moves
to one of the tables.
Boys look over the dead man
at the empty chair.

Chuck 4.25.01

BETTY REMEMBERS:

I first came over for an interview for a job on January, 2005. Chuck had just got out of the hospital and had told me he almost died. He was very unkempt. Corky was taking care of him. He was not getting bathed & wasn't taking his medication right at all, so, all things considered I wasn't going to take the job. Chuck was mean and unruly, especially when I told him I wouldn't be able to start until 9:30 in the morning. After a couple of days, I called him back about the position and he said that we would give it a try. Corky said he didn't want to do it anymore. So now there was only me! Chuck was so sick. I came on board and changed his life for the better. He reluctantly started getting bathed regularly and he now was dressing better and had clean clothes to wear. I paid attention to his diet as the Dr. started filling me in on a lot of his dietary needs (no more Dr. Pepper, etc.). He started taking his medication the right way and became less disoriented and eventually started walking without a walker and then later (about 6 months later) he didn't even need his cane. Now he was the Chuck everyone told me about, a real asshole! As time went on, Chuck started realizing that I knew what I was doing.

Chuck started seeing Dr. Garcia, the liver transplant doctor and was put on the actual transplant list and he had already quit alcohol but he didn't realize that meant marijuana, too. He had to wait another 3 months and try to stop smoking. Well, we know how that went. Then they added another 3 months and so on. Chuck had a great reason for smoking pot. "I'm retired—why not?"

Chuck started feeling better and he was around a little longer and he could meet his granddaughter for the first time just a few months before he passed on.

We went to Gold Country, stayed in the hotel, and being quite the penny-pincher that he was, that was a big splurge. We saw a band that he really liked, "Asleep At The Wheel". We had a blast.

Shortly after this, he started feeling more and more sick, the beers didn't help, that's what caused his health to go down hill.

He said he would take care of me and he did by making sure I had his little apartment (me and my cat!). He said he was going out with a "bang" on his 60th birthday and have a kegger and all his family and friends around, but he didn't make it that far. Last thing he said to me was, "I love you, Betty, with all my heart, and I'll be smiling at you from the other side."

Betty James
Friend, Care-Giver
Chico, CA, May 27, 2008

FOUR FOR THE ROAD

Chuck didn't drive, he was never at risk of a DUI, but whenever he was a passenger of mine, at whatever time of day, he would take a beer with him, or however many were required to make the journey at hand. One For The Road *might have been his motto. One day in the summer of 2006, Chuck's last summer, I got a call from Corky. Chuck had just experienced a serious relapse episode and was back in the hospital. I drove up to Chico and visited but Chuck was weak and confused and we didn't talk much. When I drove home it was with the expectation that I would not see him alive again, but somehow he recovered sufficiently to be sent home and I drove back up. He was shuffling about his little house and was proud to tell me that before his recent relapse he had actually had the strength to walk a block to the corner and back. "Yeah? That's great!" I said, and at the pace of his shuffle it* was *quite a feat. "Yeah," he said, "I walked to the corner and bought four cans of beer and walked back and drank them all! The next morning I woke up ice-cold, shivering, unable to move. Corky found me and called 911. Do you think the Doctors found the alcohol in my blood?" "Probably," I said. "Well," he said, "guess I won't be getting a new liver now! Funny thing is they didn't even taste good!" He smiled at the irony of that.*

Gene

Last Christmas, 59th Birthday, East 9th St., Chico, 2005

With Zach, Last Birthday & Christmas, Chico, 2005

Really I didn't know Chuck too well. I knew he was my father's brother...my uncle, and that his wife's name was Buttons. I started hearing more about him, though, as he got sick and I heard his wife passed.

My dad and I went up to see him in Chico for his birthday toward the end. He had long grey hair and long fingernails and his hands shook, but I could see in his eyes that he was all there. He had no problem smiling and though he seemed pretty tired he enjoyed the company and conversation. He actually seemed at peace, more so than most people you pass on the street or stand behind in line at the bank.

Well, that was the last time I saw him and I'm glad I did. It was good to see a man at peace.

Zach Hudson, nephew
San Francisco, May 19, 2008

On The River, Chico, Christmas 2005

GOING TO SLEEP

It was Aug 23rd, 2006. Chuck had by now accepted the fact that there would be no miracle recovery. It was just a matter of time and not much of it. He wanted to die in his own bed in his little rented house a mile away on E. 9th St. where he and Buttons had spent her final days. He lay now in the hospital bed attached to wires and tubes. His family and friends stood around while the Doctor explained what would soon happen. He told Chuck his blood pressure was so weak it could not sustain itself, that a fluid going into his arm was all that kept the pressure up and him alive. He said when the tube was removed his blood pressure would decline rapidly and the end would come. He asked Chuck if he understood what this meant. Chuck said, "It means I'll die." The Doctor said, "Yes, do you understand when?" "When? Well, not anytime soon. Not like tomorrow." The doctor hesitated. He said, "Sooner, Chuck, much sooner. The fluid is very powerful. It is keeping you alive. When we remove the tube your blood pressure will drop and you will go to sleep. You will close your eyes and it will be just like going to sleep. Do you understand this? I can't authorize your release to go home unless you tell me that you understand this."

275

It was at this precise point that Chuck was forced to free himself from the denial that had been his last defense against death these past several days. It was very quiet in the room. You could see and feel the ultimate acceptance that chuck struggled to arrive at. Though all hearts were with him at that moment, no one could help him arrive at that vast comprehension. He was alone, the way he had come into this world, the way he was about to leave it. All the many words he had spoken and written about death were now just so many words in the face of this reality. He looked around at each of us, then back at the Doctor. He said, "I understand."

It was arranged that Chuck would be brought by gurney to an ambulance, then to his house. He would remain attached to his tubes till the ambulance arrived, then the attendants would pull them and wheel him inside and remove him from the gurney and lay him on his bed. Then the hospice people would take over. This was an insurance concern. The hospital could not be responsible for Chuck's well-being once he exited the ambulance; therefore the tubes had to be pulled first. Hence he would lose precious final living moments between exiting the ambulance, being wheeled in on his gurney, then being laid on his bed. It was necessary that everyone who wanted to be with him at the final moment must arrive at the house before the ambulance, in time for the Really Big Show. *It was getting absurd; I think Chuck felt the absurdity. He might have been having second thoughts about dying at home, if he had to race against time to do it. Did he want to spend his last moments the focal point of a spectacle? He might have been asking himself, as he had so many times in his life: What's the point?*

Before we left the room, Chuck raised his hand up and regarded it with a kind of affection. He opened and closed his fingers, watching them: he was saying goodbye to his own flesh. We looked into each other's eyes, deeper than we ever had. We shook hands. We squeezed...hard, harder. He was wasted away, but his grip was like iron. I said, "You're strong!" He said, "Not as strong as you!" Those were our last words.

Coordinating the ambulance and the attendants and the hospice people would take a few hours. We were all to go have some lunch or whatever and reconvene at Chuck's at 2:00 pm. I went with Chuck's daughters, Tris and Katie, to Lunch. We went to a pizza joint. We ordered beer. We didn't say much. We had a second beer. Tris's cell phone rang. She listened, we waited.

"Thank you," she said and hung up and her eyes told us Chuck was gone. We three held hands across the table and cried.

We went into his room and said our silent farewells. I touched his hand, his foot, the hair on his face. He was in peaceful repose, just not there. An hour ago he was there, now he wasn't. I didn't know what that meant; it was beyond comprehension. I went out and up to the nurse who had been so helpful and sympathetic the last several days. I tried not to cry. She said, "He went peacefully. I was in the room. He said to me, 'It's been nice knowing you.' I said to him, 'Thank you, Chuck, I'll see you again.' He said, 'No, I'm going to sleep now.' I said, 'Good, you should get some rest, I'll be back soon.' He said, 'You don't understand: I'm going to sleep now,' and he closed his eyes and when I came back into the room moments later, he was gone."

Chuck was cremated and his ashes portioned out, some to Pacific Grove and Chico, California; some to Kentucky and Tennessee; some to Freeburg, Missouri. A small memorial was held in Chico, in the yard of Erica Mclane, where some of his ashes were buried and an avocado tree planted on the spot.

January, 2007, a small gathering of Luetkemeyers in Freeburg, Missouri, where a portion of Chuck's ashes were buried in Holy Family cemetery alongside the grave of his father and his father's father.

I am the winter of my death
　　　　but not an ending
　　a waiting, stillness of waiting
guardian of seeds
　　　　in frozen earth
the storms fall in silence
　　　　there is no color
　　white now, unseen
　　　　still waiting—

But a knowing
　　a turn of cycles
the turn of time
　　back on itself
stillness gives way to
　　movement
green pushes through
　　　　the earth
　　gives way to flowers
death passes into birth
　　& I am—

　　　　　　Chuck

"I didn't know how much I loved Chuck (for reasons better left unsaid) until I went to Chico to "take care of him." We had our last of many fights there. I had no illusions about his future, I knew he would die soon, but I was content with the outcome of my visit. I learned what I needed to know about him and our long tumultuous relationship: He was a lost, unhappy, bitter, even irredeemable soul stuck on earth, trying to atone for sins of another time and place. He could have done better. Part of my own soul has gone with him."

Alex St. Germaine, Sister
San Diego, CA, May 7, 2008

I will not be returning to Chico, there is nothing there for me, I will not be attending whatever stupid drunk-fest memorial they're planning on in October. As far as Chuck is concerned, we're fine by each other and he certainly understands.

Katie

You know I really miss him. It almost made me ill myself to see him sick in the hospital. He was as tough as nails for as long as I knew him.

Damien Owen, Nephew
Redding, CA, June 4, 2008

I wish that I had known him like you did. It's a huge loss in my life. I miss him...I miss everybody.

Sandy Parillo, Sister
New York, November 1, 2008

I'm glad Sean, Travis & myself made the venture to see Chuck in the hospital. It was the last time we saw him alive and before we left his hospital room, Chuck & I hugged and our lips met and I guess that was our farewell miss.

Michele

COUNTY OF BUTTE

202 MIRA LOMA DRIVE
OROVILLE, CALIFORNIA 95965

CERTIFICATE OF DEATH 3 2 0 0 6 0 4 001631

NAME OF DECEDENT — FIRST	CHARLES
MIDDLE	BERNARD
LAST	LUETKEMEYER
DATE OF BIRTH	12/25/1946
AGE	59
SEX	MALE
DATE OF DEATH	08/23/2006
HOUR	1425
BIRTH STATE/FOREIGN COUNTRY	ILLINOIS
SOCIAL SECURITY NUMBER	348-38-5577
EVER IN U.S. ARMED FORCES	YES
MARITAL STATUS	WIDOWED
RACE	WHITE
EDUCATION	SOME COLLEGE
LEGAL OCCUPATION	CHEF
KIND OF BUSINESS OR INDUSTRY	RESTAURANT
YEARS IN OCCUPATION	20

RESIDENCE

DECEDENT'S RESIDENCE	552 EAST 9th STREET
CITY	CHICO
COUNTY	BUTTE
ZIP CODE	95928
YEARS IN COUNTY	25
STATE/FOREIGN COUNTRY	CALIFORNIA

INFORMANT'S NAME, RELATIONSHIP	TRISTESSA LUETKEMEYER HOWARD (DGHT)
MAILING ADDRESS	898 FIRESIDE DRIVE, COOKEVILLE, TN 38501

SPOUSE AND PARENT INFORMATION

NAME OF FATHER — FIRST	CHARLES
MIDDLE	BERNARD
LAST	LUETKEMEYER
BIRTH STATE	MO
NAME OF MOTHER — FIRST	CLARE
LAST	YARSINSKY
BIRTH STATE	WI

FUNERAL DIRECTOR / LOCAL REGISTRAR

DISPOSITION DATE	08/26/2006
PLACE OF FINAL DISPOSITION	RES: EUGENE LUETKEMEYER, 49 TULE COURT, CLAYTON, CA 94517
TYPE OF DISPOSITION	CR/RES — NOT EMBALMED
NAME OF FUNERAL ESTABLISHMENT	NEPTUNE SOCIETY OF NO CA FD-1440
SIGNATURE OF EMBALMER	Mark U Lundberg MD MP
DATE	08/25/2006

PLACE OF DEATH

PLACE OF DEATH	MT ENLOE MEMORIAL HOSPITAL
COUNTY	BUTTE
FACILITY ADDRESS	WEST 5th AVENUE & ESPLANADE
CITY	CHICO

CAUSE OF DEATH

Cause	Interval
IMMEDIATE CAUSE: Lactic Acidosis	3 Days
Multiple Organ System Failure	3 Days
End Stage Liver Disease	Unknown
Ethanol Abuse	Unknown
OTHER SIGNIFICANT CONDITIONS: None	
WAS OPERATION PERFORMED: No	
DEATH REPORTED TO CORONER	YES
BIOPSY PERFORMED	YES
AUTOPSY PERFORMED	YES
D06-1152	

PHYSICIAN'S CERTIFICATION

DECEDENT ATTENDED SINCE	08/23/2006
DECEDENT LAST SEEN ALIVE	08/23/2006
PHYSICIAN NAME, ADDRESS	RICHARD FRIEDEN MD, 1531 Esplanade, Chico, CA 95926
LICENSE NUMBER	A-89938
DATE	08/24/2006

CORONER'S USE ONLY

MANNER OF DEATH	
FAX AUTH. #	# 1388

This is to certify that the attached is a true and correct copy of the vital record which is on file in this office of which I am legal custodian.

DATE ISSUED 08/29/2006

MARK A. LUNDBERG, M.D., M.P.H.
HEALTH OFFICER

000124070

This copy is not valid unless prepared on engraved border, displaying the date, seal and signature of the County Health Officer.

The Many Faces Of Chuck

FIGHTING DEATH

Life is for living,
    Time, with its past & future,
        is for dying—

I'll fight you, Death,
    all the way,
        I'll fight you—

But knowing
    that in the end you must win,
I'll lay down with you
    as with an old friend—

As old friends, I'll lie with you
    but from this union
        comes another life—

A dead tree becomes soil
    for the seedlings of his living,
so my dying becomes soil
    for the children of my living—

I'll not fear you, Death,
    I'll not try to run away,
but wrestle gladly with you
    to feel the strength
        of my living—

Chuck 11.10.71

MANY THANKS

□□□
Many thanks
to Erica for hosting
the Chico memorial
and for the hole in her backyard.
Many thanks to Aunt Sandy for hosting
the Freeburg Memorial and to all the good
Luetkemeyers of Missouri for welcoming Chuck home.
Many thanks to Betty for the care and companionship
she provided during Chuck's final days.
Many thanks to Katie for telling it like it is,
or how she perceives it to be,
which is the same in the end.
Many thanks to Luke for
the cover design and the full color
composite interior photograph,
The Many Faces Of Chuck.
Many thanks to Alejandro
for the innumerable PDF
conversion attempts.
Many thanks to Leslie
for so patiently waiting.
And to all who contributed
with their hearts and minds…
many thanks.
□□□